THE INVISIBLE
FORCE OF MUSIC

Tapping into your Mind and
Heart Potential for Performance Music

Paulina Derbez

"As a composer deeply Immersed in the transformative power of music, I was deeply affected by Paulina Derbez's 'The Invisible Force of Music.' This book is a moving exploration into how music can tap into our mind and heart, unlocking potentials in performance and beyond. Derbez delves into the mystical force of sound, providing insightful guidance on establishing a profound, authentic relationship with music, which transcends mere entertainment to become a transcendental experience for both performers and audiences. 'The Invisible Force of Music' is not just a guide; it's a journey to discovering one's true artistic capabilities and connecting with the mystical dimension of music. It's a must-read for anyone eager to explore the deeper realms of musical art and its impact on humanity."

Barry Goldstein, Multi Award Winning Composer, Producer and Best-Selling Author

"With this book Derbez invites us on a journey of reflection to view the experience of practicing a musical instrument from a complex, transdisciplinary perspective. Over the course of its different chapters, she maintains a constant focus on taking conscious and integral control of our own artistic activity, with the metacognitive regulation necessary to perform our music effectively.
With an inspiring and practical style, Derbez brings us closer to the invisible force in music, always anchored in specific, practical exercises. Maintaining a profound and consistently pedagogical approach throughout, she intentionally strikes a beautiful balance between the mental, the emotional and the physical.
This is without doubt an indispensable book for musicians and music educators alike. "

Dr. Miguel Angel Cano, Coordinator of the Master's program in pedagogy at the School of Music of Catalonia (ESMUC).

"I profoundly believe that expressing and sharing the magic of music extends beyond playing skills and involves an intimate connection with one's true self. Paulina's profound insights and compelling exploration inspire a journey to rediscover the authentic essence of artistic creation and invite us to explore, through it, the deeper purpose of our existence."

Aline Champion 1st Violin, Berliner Philharmoniker Professor, Geneva Music University Director, Villars Music Academy Psychotherapist (HP)

"In the book The Invisible Force of Music Paulina Derbez proposes her new methodology for learning music. She does so by first drawing the reader in through a brief narration of her days as a violin student, then by exposing her difficulties in learning her much loved instrument. In laying bear her vulnerabilities, the reader is won over, feeling compelled to read on. In this guide to a new way of approaching and experiencing music, Derbez takes us through achieving balance and awareness of the body, creating an emotional connection to the music, and the importance of connecting with the audience during performance. The tone of the book is honest and unassuming. Its language is simple and clear. Nonetheless, The Invisible Force of Music touches on important topics in music research."

Berenice Beverley Zammit, Performance Guru

"Embark on a transformative journey with Paulina Derbez's compelling book, "The Invisible Force of Music." In this thought-provoking exploration, Derbez goes beyond the confines of conventional music discourse, passionately asserting that music can and should lead the way for a profound cultural transformation. Derbez echoes the belief that musicians, as the custodians of this invisible force, hold the power to infuse coherence and depth not only within themselves but also in the hearts of their audience.

"The Invisible Force of Music" doesn't just spotlight the responsibility musicians bear to connect with their art; it advocates for the creation of a coherent heart in both performers and listeners alike. Derbez's work becomes a catalyst for positive change, emphasizing the symbiotic relationship between music and healing. Practical exercises and step-by-step guidance within the pages of this book serve as a roadmap for musicians at every stage of their journey – from aspiring students seeking deeper insights into healthy practice techniques to seasoned professionals yearning to rediscover wholesome perspectives on music practice and the broader musical landscape.

Derbez's vision extends beyond the rehearsal room, envisioning a future where the transformative power of music permeates society. This book serves as a manifesto for those eager to unlock the invisible force within music, not just as a means of personal expression but as a force capable of fostering unity, understanding, and healing in a world that desperately needs it. "The Invisible Force of Music" stands as a testament to the belief that the music world should not only reflect our aspirations but actively guide us towards a more harmonious and connected existence."

Dr. Mercedes Diaz Garcia, Orchestra Conductor

"Paulina Derbez, as a recognized violinist and teacher, offers us a profoundly revealing and inspiring book that will surely open the minds of all music teachers and students who have the good fortune to read it. This is no user's manual with technical instructions and standard strategies, but a text that views teaching and learning a musical instrument as a completely holistic, comprehensive and gratifying process, in which mind, body and emotions are integrated synergically to engage with music on its most absolutely communicative and human level. To do this, it is essential for the teacher to become a credible, personal role model, not a mere *transmitter of knowledge*, but a guide who supports students with carefully researched scientific and psycho-pedagogical knowledge in the complex and challenging process of becoming a good performer.

One of the most excruciating dimensions traditionally associated with learning an instrument in the field of classical music is the fear of making a mistake, as if everything revolved around an objective of technical perfection as a sole and exclusive priority. Standards for learning an instrument focus primarily on technical proficiency from the perspective of deficiency, giving rise to learning processes associated with negative emotions and suffering. This narrow view of learning, which operates with the implicit idea of the "you'll get it all right in the end" technique (for those who "get it right," of course), is not only obviously obsolete and invalid, but also prone to triggering an adverse process that may well lead to giving up music. It is a back-to-front world. Music, as a primordial human practice and field of knowledge, should always be associated with satisfaction, happiness and communication, where technique has its rightful place as a means to the end of achieving musicality, to express emotions—not emotions of anxiety or anguish, but of fulfillment and artistic sensibility.

Derbez proposes an approach founded on a profoundly humanistic vision of music teaching from the point of view of her own experience in her life's journey of transformation as a performer and a teacher, exploring the most relevant current perspectives ranging from neuroscience to positive psychology, and prioritizing the analysis of the emotional and cognitive states that condition and monitor the processes of performing music. Her ideas related to the importance of techniques of meditation, attribution, visualization, relaxation and metacognitive reformulation, based on techniques like heart coherence, alert us to the vital importance of training musicians to reformulate their thoughts, emotions and expectations, to believe in themselves, and ultimately to achieve self-control, self-regulation and professional empowerment."

Josep Zaragozá, ESMUC (Catalonia College of Music)

"Paulina's book is an indispensable guide for both performing musicians and music educators, delving into a question rarely asked but profoundly important: "Why do I do this?" The answer to this inquiry resides deep within the artist's heart. By aligning one's passion with purpose, it not only fuels the drive to excel as a musician but also equips with the essential tools for reaching their full potential.

Paulina's book serves as an illuminating compass, ushering musicians towards an intimate connection with the music they perform. It fosters the harmonious flow of positive energy coursing through their very being, enabling transformative thoughts and words to shape their musical journey. It also encourages the realization that musicians are integral to the grand tapestry of life and nature on our planet, and their music carries a significant contribution to this symphony of existence.

Through this book, I have gained invaluable insights that have not only elevated my musical abilities but have also enriched my overall well-being. It's a transformative resource that has empowered me to become a more fulfilled individual."

Frank Horvat, Composer

"Early on in her beautiful book, Paulina writes," *There are moments in life when we make decisions without knowing exactly where they might lead, yet we follow them through because we feel that they are what we need to grow, that they are an inner call to change our paths.* Trusting this truth, Paulina continues to grow as an artist and inspires others to do the same. The exercises she shares within these pages apply not only to those who desire expansive development of their musicianship and artistry but are also applicable for those who wish to open and lift their capacity for grounded, open - hearted presence in their day to day lives, as well. I have had the privilege of collaborating with Paulina - as a stage director and also as a dramaturg on a recent project. I continue to be inspired by her desire for mining ever deeper truths and breath in her work - and in herself. Paulina's writing shares all of herself: her honesty, her humility, her generosity, her insight, her pedagogy, practices, expertise, wisdom, personal stories, and artistic journeys, all of it informed by her expansive and loving heart. This is Paulina."

Liza Balkan, Theatre and Opera Director, Librettist, Writer, and Educator.

"After the isolation of the pandemic, it is time to question and reimagine our approach to music. In this compelling book, Derbez takes us on an inner journey to create music from the source of creativity within our own minds, hearts, and souls. She offers effective, powerful tools to build technique and musicality not merely from exterior modeling, but from our own inexhaustible wellspring of imagination. This book is an excellent road map for those seeking deeper meaning and purpose in their music. This "inside-out" approach brings not only rapid musical progress, but healing and connection as well."

David Eby, cellist, educator, lecturer, and writer

AOS PUBLISHING, 2024

AOS POETRY, 2024

ISBN: 978-1-990496-62-2
Translation by: Martin Boyd

Cover Design: Chanelle Poupart

Visit AOS Publishing's website:
www.aospublishing.com

Acknowledgements

This book has been made possible by the support of wonderful people who have contributed in different ways with their knowledge and experience. First of all, I would like to thank all my professors in the Master's program in Music Pedagogy at Escola Superior di Música di Catalunya in Barcelona, especially my thesis advisor, Dr. Javier Duque Gutiérrez, and the professors Josep Lluís Zaragoza Muñoz, Dr. Luis García Vázquez, Rubén Bes Rams, Dr. Miguel Angel Cano, Ignasi Gómez Margarit, and Vika Kleiman. I would also like to thank Irena Portenko and my students Rosa Romero and Rogerio Pérez. I would like to thank my husband, Martin Boyd, for his unconditional support, and my daughter, Isabella, for being an inspiration for growth and the source of so much joy.

To my parents Silvia and Jorge

Table of Contents

Preface

Music has the power to transform anyone who lets it into their heart. It is a path to a healing that can be physical, mental, or emotional. For this to happen, both musicians and listeners need to tune into the invisible energy of the world of sound. We can do this by connecting with its purest and highest essence. All we need to do is open our hearts to its virtues so as to receive its infinite, powerful love. In this way, we can connect our soul to the source of music so that it can fulfil its mission for humankind.

Over the years, I have discovered that the world of sound is located in a place beyond space and time. It is permeated with a mystical force that can connect us to our true power as human beings. For this to happen, in addition to establishing a profound and authentic relationship with their art, players of musical instruments must guide the audience to receive their art by expressing it from the depths of their hearts. In this way, the music can transform a mere event of entertainment into a transcendental moment for both the performer and the audience. The space, the artist, the music, and the audience will become a single, unbreakable unit.

The objective of this book is thus to offer you the chance to establish a healthy and creative relationship with music and with your musical instrument through principles based on mental, emotional, and physical metacognition. These principles will be applied to your daily instrument practice, in order to turn stage fright into an experience of maximum musical expression and to turn a musical event into a space of true transformation. At the same time, this book proposes a new methodology for learning a musical instrument, based on a new vision of music.

This book is divided into three parts. The first proposes the theory behind the main educational principles, the second applies those principles to practice with specific activities, and the third describes a new format for concerts where the music can serve as a means of real transformation and healing for performers and listeners alike.

The seed of this new methodology was sown several years ago, in a beautiful town called Lugano. I invite you to step back with me to that moment.

Once upon a time...

There are moments in life when we make decisions without knowing exactly where they might lead, yet we follow them because we feel that they are necessary for us to grow, that they are an inner call to change our paths as human beings and as artists. This is just what happened to me at the age of nineteen, when I decided to pack my bags and follow that voice called intuition. In January 1993, I boarded a flight that took me from Mexico, where I had lived my whole life until then, to a place called Lugano in the Swiss Alps.

Lugano is a small city located in the Italian part of Switzerland, surrounded by lakes and mountains. It is a truly beautiful city and was without doubt the perfect location to begin the personal and professional development of that stage of my life.

I was picked up at the airport by the man who would be my violin teacher for the next three years and, without knowing it, the key person who contributed to the creation of a new form of studying and perceiving the world of music.

After a while I began to feel better adapted to the place and to my new situation. The classes with my new teacher were going well. In the first six months he worked exclusively on improving my technique, as he did with all his students. It was the first time that a teacher had given me real technical training, which would be fundamental to my development as a violinist and a teacher. At that time, I was living with a very kind Italian family and living off a scholarship to pursue my studies at the conservatory. Everything seemed to be going so well.

When I had finished the term dedicated exclusively to technique, my teacher assigned me a piece of music to play. I then returned to Mexico for two months, where I had to prepare the piece for the next academic term. It was at that moment that I realized that I didn't know how to study! The more I repeated the piece, one way or another, my mental and physical tensions seemed to pile up.

In this way, preparing the piece was almost impossible, because all the problems with my way of studying prior to my term of technique began rearing their ugly heads, one after another. I had no idea how to resolve them. I was also terrified by the thought of returning to Switzerland because I knew, in the depth of my being, that on arriving in Lugano I would have to climb a huge mountain: I would have to face the fact that I did not know how to study. Despite this fear, I felt I had to go back. Once more I listened to the voice of intuition, which led me to take the flight back to Lugano.

On my second arrival in Switzerland, everything was different. I was not living with the nice Italian family anymore; instead, I was sharing a house with some other students, who were hardly ever there. I felt very lonely, sad, and terrified by the thought of climbing that big mountain that loomed ever closer.

My study method in those days consisted mainly of repeating the musical passages over and over, playing them slower and then faster, or vice versa. I had no idea at all about how to use my mental, emotional, and physical metacognitive capacities in my daily study. I knew nothing about these things. As a result, I suffered severe muscular tensions, arising from a lack of mental and emotional clarity, and the absence of an effective study method, whenever I played violin.

This was my situation when I arrived at my first class of the term with my teacher. I felt terribly nervous and fearful of making a mistake. And I did; I began making one mistake after another. This scene was repeated in subsequent classes, pushing my desire to study down to the floor.

For my teacher it was a given that I had to arrive to class with the material well prepared, like all the other students who studied in his classes, which were always open to the public. But for me, the reality was very different. I had no idea how to tackle a piece to achieve the result he expected. This made me feel frustrated and sad both in class and in my practice at home. It was as if my true inner force was asleep. My apparent lack of preparation began to exasperate my teacher and turned most of my classes with him into torture for both of us. Nevertheless, it was thanks to this difficult period of my life as a student that my mind began to wake up. I realized that I was not playing as well as I really could and that I had to do something about it. I thus began a period of searching that led me to my goal: the creation of a new study method that would teach me to play with my true artistic potential and with a new vision of the music as a path to healing.

Due to the tension I developed at that time with my teacher in Lugano, I suffered an injury in one of my hands that forced me to stop playing violin for two months. At that time, I focused on healing my hand using alternative therapies such as the Alexander Technique, and I took a course in eurythmic dance (Rudolf Steiner, 1861-1925). Fortunately, I felt more relaxed because it was summer vacation, which allowed me to take things slowly and dedicate my time to myself and my own recovery.

On one of those summer days, I was walking down the street, reflecting on why I suffered so much tension when I played, and wondering what was keeping me from enjoying my daily study. Suddenly, the following thought came into my head:

"Every technical or musical problem is resolved first at the mental level."

It was a glorious moment for me. I had hit the key that would start me off on a total renewal of my personal study technique. I felt happy, because I knew right then that a change was beginning. It was a change that would transform not only my way of studying but also my way of teaching and experiencing music.

After that moment of revelation, I went back to my home. I took my violin in my hands and began to play. At that moment, I heard my teacher's voice in my head. I realized that his attitude towards me was so strong that I had made it part of my musical reality. His way of judging me had become my form of self-criticism. I knew at that moment that it was time to change how I saw myself as an artist and to take back my own creative power on mental and emotional levels.

I closed my eyes and was surprised to see myself playing tense! Of course, the fact that everybody was telling me that I was too stiff when I played had made my mind register it as a total and absolute truth. My system of beliefs, consolidated in my subconscious mind, had taken the judgements of those around me and internalized them as my physical reality as a violinist. I tried to improve this "reality" with external solutions like lowering my shoulders when I played or studying technical challenges like *vibrato* a thousand different ways. But these solutions weren't enough, because they were only temporary, and they limited my potential instead of developing it.

The realization that I saw myself as a tense violin player led me to the decision that I had to change my mental image of who I was when I played my musical instrument. It was clear that the problems that arose during my classes were the result of my way of studying, and the mental programming that I had in relation to my vision as an artist. It was time to change that programming and my system of beliefs.

It was a very revealing moment for me. It was as if something inside me had collapsed. But this internal collapse left room for a new way of looking at and resolving any apparent challenge in my creative musical process. From then on, I began to apply this new vision when I practised violin each day. It was a vision where the application of my mental potential constituted a revolutionizing element in my daily practice, and I began solving every problem I faced in my playing first on the mental level. In other words, I began "mentally picturing" each solution to each challenge before playing it on the violin.

At that time, I had the good fortune to meet the woman who would become my teacher for the following two and a half years. Meeting my new teacher marked a new beginning for me. Finally, I started to find my own way of studying. I realized that the solution to any problem comes from within; that is, from my own mental and emotional power.

All the physical and emotional tensions I'd suffered until then in my playing were simply the result of negative thoughts and feelings caused by my lack of understanding how to study, and by giving my power over my way of playing the violin to the opinions of others. Yet I am eternally grateful to those people, because they helped awaken my true inner power and find a new way, a way that has been of benefit both to me and to everyone who has used the strategies of discovery that form part of this new method of studying music.

Of course, the results were not immediate, as like anything else, practice and determination are needed to achieve your goal. Studying in this way meant that I had to start exercising my mental muscle in order to achieve optimal results. However, even if the effects were not that obvious in the beginning, one thing that was clear was that I finally began to enjoy studying violin. My mind had relaxed.

The emotional padlock that had kept it shut for so long had now been opened, allowing ideas to flow and express themselves naturally on the physical level. In other words, this opening had a positive effect on my physical condition, and I began to feel free of tension when I played violin. I rediscovered and reconciled with the world of sound and with the medium through which I could express the depths of my being. Since then, I've been constantly amazed to discover the capacities lying within every artist, both students and professionals, and the power that can be unleashed when one makes the conscious decision to give the most of oneself.

Another revelation for me was the recognition of the power of the emotions and how they are profoundly influenced by our thoughts. I remember that one thing my teacher repeatedly demanded was that I play with more expression. Well, of course... but how? How could I be more expressive if the one emotion that dominated my classes and study in those days was a terrifying fear of making a mistake? And anyway, what did my teacher mean by playing with more expression? Did he mean that I had to use more bow or more *vibrato*? Or to play louder? Or to loosen up, to enjoy the music more? No doubt his intentions were good, but saying something like this without further explanation puts students on a road to nowhere. Once I became aware of all this, I realized that I needed to find an effective way to become more expressive in every sense of the word. A way that would give my playing a conscious and profound expressiveness.

In those days, I often took walks through the beautiful forests in that part of Switzerland. I would spend hours contemplating the natural beauty that surrounded me, listening to its sounds and breathing in its scents. I remember that I had a special spot at the foot of a huge oak tree. Being there gave me a sense of peace and safety; it was like a refuge where I could be with myself. I would often take my violin there and study while surrounded by the magic of nature. One day when I'd gone there without my violin, I began playing without my instrument. That is, I made the movements with my arms as if I were playing, but without the physical presence of the violin. I played a melody in my head. This had the effect of opening up my emotions in an extraordinary way, so that I could feel the emotive force that lay within me. The creative centre of my heart opened up in a wonderful and profound way.

At that moment, I was struck by another revelation: to be expressive, I needed to feel the specific emotion that I wanted to emanate through the music. Indeed, to feel the emotive force of the music within me in the midst of the silence of the forest was a much more powerful experience than listening to the sound outside me. I felt that the world of sound was alive inside me. My emotional field, my conscious expressive force, was awoken.

From that day, I thus began to associate music with the world of nature. I found that by doing this I could attain a more expressive experience of the music itself. By mentally evoking an element of nature when I played, I found that this created a specific feeling within me, which I could emanate naturally and consciously in my playing. I realized that "playing with more expression" meant experiencing a specific emotion, which would lead to the natural creation of the sounds that represented that emotion. And in this way, I could allow a powerful energy flow from my heart whenever I played the violin. I found a bridge of energy between myself and the world of sound.

At the same time, my body began to react differently when I played my instrument. My muscles began to relax and to find the physical energy I needed to play the piece in question. My body began to respond gratefully because it was being guided by my mind and my emotions. I realized that the real solutions to our problems arise from within and not from without.

I also became aware of the fundamental importance of the latent connection between mind, emotions, and body when we play an instrument, and how this connection depends totally on the quality of the balance we achieve between these three elements. It is through this balance that we can accomplish the true mission of music: to transform ourselves.

From that moment, my ability and my confidence as a violinist began to improve significantly. At the same time, the desire to share this new vision of music led me to create a new methodology for music practice, called the Conscious Musician. This methodology is a combination of holistic teaching practices that I have been teaching now for more than twenty years, in Switzerland, Mexico, Canada, Costa Rica, and Austria, both to children and to advanced students and music professionals. Over this time, I have witnessed excellent results thanks to the creative power that lies in each student and the power of music, as it helps the students to become their own best teachers at home when practising with their musical instrument.

This book tells the story of the creation of this new methodology and vision of music. It is a vision that leads everyone who is open to it to experience the world of sound consciously and apply their true potential to their art. It is a vision that not only offers studying strategies, but also proposes a different way of perceiving the world of music and of expressing that world in a more authentic and pure way, allowing the music to manifest its true mission: to guide our feelings to their purest and highest essence and help us rediscover our mission as creators of the world of sound.

This rediscovery has the power to help all those who decide to apply it to play their musical instrument free of tension and with the full use of their real potential as an artist and a performer. In this way, their mission can be accomplished, and they can achieve a profound connection with their audience, thus turning a musical event into a site of transformation.

This book is also a guide for students with the intention of transforming a part of themselves through music. It is a way of seeing music as a path to healing both for us as artists and for our audiences. It is here that perceiving the world of sound from the creative centre of your heart can become an effective strategy both in your daily practice and in the mission of classical music in the world today.

May the magic of the world of sound and rhythm guide you down the new paths that you wish to follow from this moment, paths that bring out your true essence as a human and as the creative being that you are. It is up to you to take the first step towards a new way of experiencing music and yourself as an artist and a messenger of the world of sound, a world that vibrates inside you at all times. With this in mind, I invite you to embark on the mission proposed in this book and thus to enrich your valuable musical journey.

Introduction

Teaching a musical instrument in today's world is a complex task that requires us to reconsider the true mission of classical music in the history of humanity. One way of rethinking that mission is by reconnecting with the true meaning of the world of sound as a path to transformation for both the performer and the audience.

Viewing the world of sound as a medium through which you can touch the hearts and souls of your audience in a conscious way can help you approach your daily practice with a clear and specific mission: to connect your essence with the source of sound so that it can permeate your being in an effective and powerful way.

This idea opens up a new direction in relation to playing a musical instrument, and to the meaning and mission of musicians on the stage and the role of their audiences. The third part of this book offers a detailed exploration of this fundamental idea for the innovation of music education and of the mission of concert music today.

This book thus addresses the implicit need for a transformation of music teaching with an impact on performing on stage. At the same time, it places an emphasis on the invisible force that lives and breathes in music, proposing a new way of releasing that power in a live performance. In this way, music is not merely a form of entertainment but an opportunity for transformation.

The Invisible Force of Music is divided into three parts. The first part outlines the theories and teaching principles of this new musical methodology, based on scientific research and on a new vision of music. These theories and principles deal with issues related to learning a musical instrument, and specifically with mental, emotional, and physical awareness in a musician's daily music practice, the interpretative process, and onstage performance.

The second part describes specific activities aimed at developing your metacognitive capacities in music practice, your emotions in relation to playing your instrument, strengthening your body as the basis for a solid and effective technique, and your true mission as an artist onstage, turning anxiety and stage fright into a powerful artistic expression. This second section of the book also outlines a series of teaching principles for music instructors.

The third part proposes a new way of listening to and experiencing classical music as a means of healing and transformation. It also explores the concept of the *coherent concert*. This book is aimed at advanced music students, teachers and professionals, and at the general public.

There is an invisible force in music, but to access it we need to find a mental, emotional, and physical balance within ourselves as artists of sound, in order to channel and express its true power on the stage. When that balance is achieved, the magnitude of music will amaze you, allowing you to discover your true artistic capacities. You will discover a new world of physical, emotional, and mental sensations related to the musical act, and you will be able to connect with the mystical dimension of the world of music. You will form a single, unbreakable unit with your art.

It is my most sincere desire that this book may offer you a new way of understanding music, enriching your work as an artist for the benefit of mankind.

SECTION 1:
THEORY

1.1. A NEW WAY OF STUDYING MUSIC

Why Do You Play a Musical Instrument?

There may be many reasons why a musical instrument has ended up in your hands. Perhaps when you were a child the sound of the violin, piano, trumpet, or some other instrument captivated you and you had an immediate desire to learn to play it. Or perhaps one of your parents felt it necessary for their child to learn to play an instrument. Whatever the reason, suddenly you found yourself holding an object designed to emit sound.

Thus, as if by magic, you were given the opportunity to discover a new form of expression, through which the very depths of your being could speak without having to say a single word. Suddenly, you were able to experience sounds that seemed to come out of nowhere to envelope you in their presence—how beautiful! Of course, for most people, all of this is unconscious; it all happened so naturally that there was no need to think about it, because in that moment you had a direct connection with the music. Your emotions were fully connected to the infinite field of the world of sound.

Alienation from the World of Music

But then, after the honeymoon, which may last longer for some than others, where did all the joy of learning an instrument go? What happened to the delight that music gave you? Suddenly, you don't feel so captivated by the world of music and you try to find any excuse to get out of practising, because it has come to feel like a chore. Your natural connection to the world of music has been broken.

What causes this alienation from the world of music, which in some cases is so sudden? What mysterious force could have broken that bond between musician and instrument? What brought about the communication breakdown between you and the world of sound? How did you suddenly lose that feeling of joy when you play? What happened?

At some point you may have asked yourself questions similar to the ones above. If so, it means that you're on the right track, because for the transformation to take place within you, the doubts and worries about your art need to be brought to light. This is something I have experienced many times. It is as if some kind of mental block needs to be broken down to make room for the birth of new ideas that can foster my artistic development in healthy and creative ways.

An Invisible Barrier

There are a number of reasons why a kind of barrier may start to grow between you and the world of music, a barrier that can be conscious or unconscious. It may be due to a mental, emotional, or physical block.

A reflection on this situation may bring to mind past events that have influenced it. One such event may be an encounter with a teacher who seemed to treat you harshly, making you feel vulnerable in your classes, and, worse still, in your everyday contact with your musical instrument. You may even have given your power to that teacher, negatively affecting your metacognitive capacities for study at that time because their opinions came to form part of your system of beliefs as an artist and a performer.

Another factor may be that at some point in time your daily practice began to turn into an obligation, into a feeling of "I have to practice" rather than a time to enjoy playing. This feeling may have generated a state of heart incoherence and, in turn, mental incoherence. The concept of heart coherence will be discussed later in this book, exploring how to create this optimal state and how it can influence your brain. In this emotional and mental state, it becomes easier to connect with the essence of the world of sound.

Another palpable factor in the process of learning a musical instrument that can distance a performer from the world of sound is the phenomenon of stage fright, which can affect both students and professionals, and may occur in any kind of public presentation. Stage fright can make you ask yourself: "Why have I invested hours of practice if I find it torture to play in public?"

Stage fright can produce a feeling of fear of making a mistake, or of being judged or criticized in public. Merely thinking about playing in front of an audience can give rise to a sensation of fear, which in turn can provoke physical tensions, because there is an intimate connection between your mind, emotions, and body. In other words, a particular thought produces a particular feeling, which in turn produces a particular action.

The phenomenon of stage fright in advanced adult students as a cause of a distancing between performer and musical instrument will be further explored, with an emphasis on the need to implement teaching programs that cover solutions to a problem that is so important in the process of learning a musical instrument.

In addition, the third part of this book will discuss the issue of classical music as a powerful pathway to healing that can completely change your experience on the stage and eradicate stage fright from your mental agenda, turning the stage into a sacred space of artistic expression and authentic connection between performer and audience. In other words, the aim is to mentally and emotionally reprogram your relationship with the stage so that the artist of sound within you can truly shine and fulfill its mission.

Stage Fright and Its Effects

Stress in advanced adult students can become so acute that it can lead them to abandon their music studies entirely. This can be due to the countless courses they have to complete, the demands of the curriculum, the hours and hours of study, auditions, competitions, anxiety, etc. Hence the importance of incorporating programs that offer solutions for two of the most complex aspects of music studies: daily practice and performance on stage. These two issues are intimately interrelated. Having effective studying strategies will have a positive impact on students' performance because the problem does not lie solely in a concert, an audition, or a public event; it lies in your daily relationship with your musical instrument and your relationship with music and the stage.

There are numerous studies that have identified the level of stress that advanced students suffer. One of these is a study conducted by a group of teachers at Zaragoza University in Spain, titled "Music Studies at Conservatories and Stage Fright in Spain" (Zarza, Casanova, and Orejudo, 2016), which provides statistics on the learning experience of post-secondary students.

> Stage fright in music students is one of the biggest problems that this population group has to deal with in their daily practice. The study of this problem in Spanish education has barely received any attention from researchers. Out of a sample of 479 post-secondary music students at Spanish institutions, around 39% suffer from levels of stage fright higher than the theoretical mean according to the survey designed specifically for evaluating stage fright in musicians. We believe that a pedagogical reflection is needed to implement suitable curriculum plans aimed at reducing these rates of stage fright. (Zarza, Casanova and Orejudo, 2016)

These statistics clearly show that one of the big problems in music education at the post-secondary level is related to daily instrument practice, and that there is a need to create programs within the curriculum that offer solutions for treating stage fright in students.

Moreover, as Zarza, Orejudo, and Casanova (2016) point out, attention to stage fright in music education is relatively new in the scientific literature. Around 80% of musicians suffer from stage fright when performing in public (Ortiz Brugués 2008; quoted by Zarza, F. J., Casanova, Ó. and Orejudo, 2016, p.1). This is obviously a very high percentage and it suggests a need to address the problem on the educational level by introducing programs that offer effective solutions for students related to their study methods and stage performance.

Anxiety over playing in public is, as defined by Salmon (1990; quoted by Zarza, F. J., Casanova, Ó. and Orejudo, 2016, p.2), an experience of anxious apprehension about a real reduction in performing abilities in a public context, to a point that prevents individuals from demonstrating their musical skills, training, or level of education. Salmon's findings are truly revealing, because stage fright effectively prevents students from being able to offer a musical performance to the best of their abilities. Instead of a moment of enjoyment and connection with an audience, it can turn into a kind of torture. This is why it is of the utmost importance to create study methods that can help students develop their true talents and to think of the stage as a space of interconnection between them, the music, and the audience.

The study conducted by Zarza, Orejudo, and Casanova (2016) is extremely revealing, not only for the high percentage of post-secondary music students who suffer from stage fright, but also for some of the testimonies documented in their research. Responses related to student attitudes toward daily practice include:

1. The more work I do to prepare for a concert, the more likely it is I'll make a serious mistake.
2. Before a concert, I never know whether I'll have a good performance.
3. During performances, I often worry that I might not make it to the end of the performance.
4. Thinking about how I'm going to be evaluated interferes with my performance.
5. Even during the most stressful performances, I feel confident that I will play well.
6. I often worry about a negative reaction from the audience.
7. Since I began my studies, I have always felt anxious about performing.
8. I worry that a poor performance could ruin my career.
9. I avoid taking on interesting performances due to anxiety.
10. Sometimes I prepare for a concert with a feeling of terror and disaster.
11. I worry so much before a performance that I can't sleep.

Apart from comment no. five, all of the above comments denote a high level of stress related to playing in public. Comment no. ten, *Sometimes I prepare for a concert with a feeling of terror and disaster,* is probably the comment that reflects the highest level of tension related to playing on stage. This comment is the most striking of all because it demonstrates that the fear of playing in public is based on the student's relationship with the stage and their everyday relationship with their instrument. The student experiences this fear constantly, and this will be detrimental even to their daily practice. Over time this can create mental, emotional, and physical tensions in the student. Cases like this one make it clear that there is a need to create new methods for teaching and learning a musical instrument.

Comment no. two, *Before a concert, I never know whether I'll have a good performance,* points to the musician's uncertainty about how they will play in a public presentation. All in all, the testimonies listed above reflect a negative system of beliefs held by students in relation to their performance on stage. But like any system of beliefs, it can be changed, and must be in order to play freely and expressively.

It is therefore essential to apply principles in daily practice that will help students use their mental, emotional, and physical capacities to the maximum. These principles need to help the student to go from "I don't know how I will play in public" to "I know how I will play this piece." In other words, they need to support the development of their own metacognitive competencies and to reprogram their mental attitudes towards playing on stage.

To do this, students need to transform themselves and their relationship with music. At the same time, daily practice at home needs to be subject to a holistic vision that can help the musician work out how they want to play a piece in public, to feel the specific emotions they wish to convey, to play their instrument with physical agility, and to have a clear intention of transformation in every performance. It is essential for musicians to transform their relationship with the stage, and to develop a new, authentic, and profound relationship with their audiences.

All these aspects related to studying a musical instrument effectively and enjoyably, turning the on-stage performance into a powerful experience, and understanding the mission of music in today's world are addressed in the solutions offered in this book, which proposes a new vision of the world of sound that is essential for the art of music to transform both performers and their listeners. The underlying objective of all this is for musicians to establish a new connection with the musical art, a connection through which they can express themselves freely, authentically, and profoundly.

The next chapter deals with psychological aspects of education in order to explain the reasons behind the teaching principles of this new music methodology and their importance for the transformation of music education today.

1.2. THE TEACHING/LEARNING PROCESS IN BEHAVIOURISM, GENETIC COGNITIVISM, AND SOCIAL CONSTRUCTIVISM

> It is necessary to abolish man as essence, as autonomy, refuge of the anthropological ignorance of history to understand the complex behaviour of each man, conditioned by his historical contingencies. (Skinner, 1972; quoted by Ferreyra and Pedrazzi 2007, p. 43)

> Education, for most people, means trying to lead the child to resemble the typical adult of his society ... But for me, education means making creators... You have to make inventors, innovators, not conformists. (Piaget 1936)

The quotes above clearly illustrate the different understandings of education and learning of behaviourism (B. F. Skinner) and genetic epistemology (Jean Piaget). The first aims to abolish the student in the learning process, while the second seeks to lead the student to become creative and innovative. These are two very different positions in the teaching and learning process.

Behaviourism

> Give me a dozen healthy children, well-formed, and my own specified world to bring them up in, and I'll guarantee to take any one at random and train him to become any type of specialist I might select – doctor, lawyer, artist, merchant-chief, and yes, even beggar-man and thief – regardless of his talents, penchants, abilities, vocations, and race of his ancestors. (Watson, 2017)

Behaviourism had its origins in the First World War. This in itself gives us an understanding of the relationship between context and student. In this context, the student undergoes experiences in which he or she is not important. The student is merely a receptacle of information with no agency. His or her function is to perform the desirable behaviour in accordance with the teaching program.

Behaviourism studies the student's behaviour. Its methodology is based on moulding that behaviour according to the requirements of the teaching program and the established desired behaviours. What matters are the objectives to be achieved by means of methods like programmed teaching, reinforcement, and task assessment. Students who "meet expectations" will be rewarded. The individual identity of students is negated for the purpose of acquiring the required knowledge of their environment. The student is viewed as a "blank slate" that can be turned into a passive being that society can control. As behaviourism sees the

18

student as a kind of machine to be filled with information, its methodology is mechanical and rigid.

It is also important to highlight the role of the teacher in this pedagogical approach. A behaviourist teacher has the main objective of imparting knowledge as determined by the school curriculum. The teacher's function is to ensure that the student memorizes the content taught and becomes an example of satisfactory behaviour. In this case, both teacher and student are controlled by the teaching system. There is no room for creativity, critical thought, or reflection. The teacher uses strategies like positive reinforcement, which encourage students to learn for the simple fact that they will be rewarded.

Genetic Epistemology

Genetic epistemology uses a methodology based on the student's cognitive field and natural genetics. The three main factors that define this methodology are: the cognitive scheme and its operations, activity, and evolutionary stages.

This methodology leads students to develop their abilities naturally and creatively based on their individual development. Creativity is a very important component in the learning process to ensure a healthy, enjoyable education.

This theoretical approach also uses the concepts of assimilation and accommodation. These concepts refer to how the lessons presented to students are assimilated into the cognitive schemes of their developmental stage and accommodated to create new cognitive schemata (Gaspar, 2012, p.36). When this happens, an adaptive "gamma" response occurs (Piaget, 1975; quoted by Pozo, 2006, p.182). The function of such responses is to create cognitive (but not emotional) conflicts. The aim of genetic epistemology is to create thinking, innovative, critical, and creative individuals.

In the field of genetic epistemology, the teacher plays a completely different role from that played by a teacher in behaviourism. The teacher is a guide for students, facilitating their natural, creative development. Teachers act as mediators between teaching content and students. They are aware of children's developmental stages and present them with content that they can internalize naturally at the right moment. They help students develop their innate capacities in a creative way.

The goal of a teacher according to this approach is to guide students to become creative and innovative individuals capable of contributing to society with their true talents. Through their attention to students' cognitive schemes, teachers help them develop their mental potential, thereby creating new and rich cognitive schemes. An educator with this perspective sees education itself as an art.

Social Constructivism

Another important development in educational theory is social constructivism, an approach created by Lev Vygotsky (1896-1934). Social constructivism views human development as a process of gradual learning in which learners play an active role, and which occurs in a specific socio-historical and cultural context.

According to Zaragozà (2017), the main principles of social constructivism in relation to the learning process are:

1. Knowledge is constructed by students themselves, who create their own unique cognitive representation. The teacher should help the student to create this representation.
2. In the development of knowledge, however it may happen, the content itself is as important as the prior knowledge and motivation to learn that students bring to the learning experience.
3. Knowledge is constructed in a cultural and social context through interaction.

Within the psychological pedagogical approach of social constructivism, there are two theories that play a fundamental role in the new practices for musical instrument teaching described in this book. These are meaningful learning and discovery learning.

Meaningful Learning

The American psychologist David Ausubel (1918-2008) was the creator of the theory of meaningful learning, which became a very important concept in the field of constructivism. Meaningful learning involves teaching students based on their previous knowledge, creating a relationship between old and new knowledge so that they can participate in the construction of the new content. In this way, students' prior knowledge is transferred to the construction of new knowledge. This is a positive transfer. The new knowledge thus becomes more meaningful to the student. In the 1960s, David Ausubel, (Biografías y Vidas, 2004), published some significant results from his studies in books like *The Psychology of Meaningful Verbal Learning* (1963) and *Educational Psychology: A Cognitive View* (1968).

> Ausubel places the emphasis on the organization of knowledge into structures and in the restructuring that occurs due to the interaction between those structures present in the individual and the new information. (Pozo, 1989; quoted by Rodríguez, 2008, p.9)

Another constructivist approach is the method of discovery learning developed by Jerome Bruner (1915-2016). One of the key features of this methodology is teaching and learning by guided discovery: the instructor should motivate students to discover relationships between concepts and construct propositions on their own. A key metaphor used in this approach is "scaffolding", which refers to the use of support structures by the teacher; as student knowledge develops, the support structures are gradually removed (Zaragozà 2017). Encouraging students to discover knowledge with the teacher's guidance motivates them and gives them a much higher level of satisfaction. It is a way for students to internalize knowledge, to make it their own so that they can apply it effectively in their environment.

Bruner developed this theory in the 1960s. At that time, discovery learning constituted a radical paradigm shift in education, because rather than merely feeding knowledge directly to students as had generally been done up until then, it would be discovered gradually by the students themselves with teacher guidance. Students are thus able to discover things actively and constructively (Valencia, 2018).

According to experts from the International University of Valencia (2018), the benefits of discovery learning include:

1. Helps to overcome the limitations of mechanistic learning.
2. Stimulates students to think for themselves.
3. Stimulates self-esteem and self-confidence.
4. Encourages creative problem solving.

It is worth noting that Ausubel also advocated the discovery learning method, although he believed it should be used only for the first developmental stages and not for mature-age students (Zaragozà 2017). However, I would argue that discovery learning is still highly effective for mature-age learners because it helps individuals to develop their metacognitive competencies, which are essential for the learning process.

The next section outlines another psychological pedagogical approach with a significant influence on the approach to learning an instrument proposed in this book: metacognition. Through metacognition, students will be able to use their true mental, emotional, and physical capacities to study more effectively and enjoyably.

Metacognition

Metacognition refers to being conscious of your own consciousness. It is related to procedural knowledge; in other words, your ability to control your cognitive processes. It involves planning what is to be learned, controlling the learning process, and evaluating the results. Etymologically, "metacognition" is a combination of the Greek prefix *meta*, meaning "above", and the Latin *cognoscere*, meaning "acquisition of knowledge". It thus refers to understanding our own process of knowledge acquisition.

Metacognition is necessary for the implementation of new educational strategies that are already having an important impact on student learning around the world. Through a metacognitive process, learners can develop abilities and strategies based on their own knowledge to solve problems in a way that is truly meaningful for themselves and their environment (Jaramilla and Simbaña, 2014). In this way, students will have effective learning strategies for their daily instrument practice because they can draw on conscious learning skills that will help them achieve optimal results in each practice. As will be demonstrated in the following chapters of this book, metacognition plays a vitally important role in the development of each of the teaching principles of the Conscious Musician methodology outlined in this book.

The next section of this chapter will connect some of the psychological pedagogical approaches outlined above with the world of music education today.

Behaviourism in Music Education Today

It is clear that behaviourism still prevails in many conservative schools of music today. Students are expected to adapt to the curriculum established by the institution. There is no questioning of whether students are learning effectively and creatively, whether the repertoire being imposed upon them is suitable for their development at the time it is assigned, whether their relationship with music is authentic and free of tension, or even whether they are enjoying their music studies. They simply must comply with the established program. The assumption is that studying an instrument six or seven hours a day based on constant repetition will produce a successful musician. These expectations make it evident that behaviourism is still alive and well in the world of classical music teaching.

It is behaviourism that prioritizes the curriculum and requires teachers to ensure that students complete it satisfactorily. Programmed learning, classroom worksheets, and task assessments are all in line with Skinner's behaviourist principles. The student is not required to reflect on the material studied, but merely to memorize the content. Students don't really interact with the content;

they are merely information receptacles. This can still be seen in music schools today, especially in more conservative institutions.

In such contexts, where the musical instrument teacher often dictates what has to be worked on without considering the student and his or her potential for reflection and metacognition, it is extremely important that educators reflect on their own pedagogical approach and transform that approach through the integration of teaching strategies, drawing on social constructivism and the concept of metacognition that treat students as thinking, sensitive individuals capable of tackling challenges in their daily practice with their instrument in creative ways. Music schools also need to update their curricula for the benefit of healthier student development. But this is an issue that could fill a whole book in itself. The objective here is merely to raise it as a point for reflection on the future of music education in institutional contexts.

Social Constructivism and Music Education

The step from behaviourism (Skinner) to genetic epistemology (Piaget) represented a giant leap forward in education. The shift from an approach that ignored the student in the learning process to one that focused on the student's creative and innovative capacities constituted an extremely important change in attitudes towards teaching and learning. Another leap forward was the product of the influence of social constructivism (Vygotsky, Ausubel, Bruner) on education. The following section considers elements of social constructivism present in music education.

Meaningful Learning and Discovery Learning in Music

Ausubel's concept of meaningful learning is diametrically opposed to repetitive learning (Duque, 2006). This contrast between these two learning strategies is key to the transformation of musical instrument teaching, in which students often simply repeat a piece over and over without understanding why. The opposite approach would be one where students are able to give meaning to their learning experience, participating in its construction and applying what they learn to their daily practice. To this end, teachers should guide them to develop their capacity for reflection on their own playing and to transfer that capacity to their daily practice. In this way, students will give meaning to what they have learned in class and be able to turn mechanical repetition into conscious, creative, and effective repetition. In other words, they will understand why they are repeating a piece, which will help them to take control of their daily study. They will become their own Michelangelo in each practice.

When studying a musical instrument, the discovery learning approach can also be extremely beneficial for students. This is because students normally spend around one hour a week with their teacher and the rest of the time, they have to practice their instrument on their own. The ability to discover solutions in their daily practice will make that practice more effective and enjoyable. Finding their own solutions will motivate them as they notice an improvement in each stage of their development as musicians. They can become their own best teacher at home. And this will happen thanks to their instructor's careful guidance. By making use of their own capacity for reflection, they will discover exactly what they want to improve in each repetition. They will develop their own ear to know what they want to hear in each musical passage. They will thus be developing their conscious listening skills, together with their mental, emotional, and physical skills to optimize their daily practice, which will have a very powerful impact on their performance on stage. Both meaningful learning and discovery learning are strategies that have been integrated into the programs of more innovative music schools, with excellent results for their students.

New Teaching Strategies for Musical Performance

One of the objectives of this book is to offer a new vision of music and a new methodology for learning a musical instrument. With this in mind, among the key elements of the Conscious Musician methodology proposed here are new learning strategies for studying a musical instrument that will help musicians to develop their mental, emotional, and physical metacognitive skills and to apply them to their daily practice and to their performances on stage. In other words, metacognition plays a primordial role in each of the learning strategies that form part of the Conscious Musician educational vision. At the same time, these strategies are also related to Ausubel's meaningful learning and to Bruner's discovery learning.

The general learning principles of the Conscious Musician methodology as they apply to playing a musical instrument, are:

1. Objectives and content aimed at developing a healthy and creative relationship with your musical instrument, with music and with the stage, through mental, emotional, and physical metacognitive processes, as well as the development of self-awareness of physical fitness for musical performance.
2. The consideration of each musician holistically, i.e., as a unique individual with their own mental, emotional, and physical capacities.
3. Attention to the importance of physical fitness as a basis for an effective and solid technique and to the development of the relationship between music and movement.

4. Conscious emotional development and the importance of heart coherence in relation to the pieces you play.
5. The ability to solve any problem while playing on the mental level through metacognitive strategies.
6. Development of your creative capacity to develop your creative competencies in relation to playing your instrument.
7. A transformation of the musician's relationship with the stage. To this end, the techniques outlined above need to be applied by musicians in a disciplined manner so that they can express their full musical and artistic potential in their performances in public.
8. Teaching techniques for musical instrument teachers that motivate students and help them to reflect on the learning process, guiding them to be better self-teachers at home.
9. Establishment of a new perception of classical music as a pathway to healing for both the performer and the listener, culminating in events like *coherent concerts.*

The Conscious Musician methodology thus provides musicians with principles to help them transform their daily practice into a work of art in itself, where they can apply their mental, emotional, and physical competencies organically and effectively. It also offers the guidelines necessary to be able to express themselves powerfully in their musical performances, transforming the hearts of those listening with their performative art in a conscious way to create new directions for live concerts.

Another objective of this book is to provide teachers with strategies that can enhance their pedagogical craft, which is so important to the student learning process. At the same time, it offers the reader a new vision of the world of sound and the art of live music and proposes a new perception of the sound artist in the world today.

In this way, *The Invisible Force of Music* will help readers create a new relationship with themselves, their musical instrument, their artistic mission, the world of sound, the stage, and the audience. It provides guidelines to create a new sonic artist within the reader.

The following chapter deals with the process of mental metacognition in one's daily practice and the power of one's mind in playing music.

1.3. THE MIND: WHERE THE TRUE SOLUTIONS DWELL

> There is only one admirable form of the imagination: the imagination that is so intense that it creates a new reality, that it makes things happen. (Sean O'Faolain, quoted in Dispenza, 2007, p. 381)

The subject of this chapter, by its very nature, raises the question: What is involved in a task as important and profound as transforming your vision of music and your daily study of a musical instrument?

The answer is that many factors are involved, including how you direct your mental potential in order to establish a new relationship with music and with yourself.

At this point perhaps you are wondering what your mental potential has got to do with playing an instrument. A lot! You play your instrument not only with your body but with your mind as well. Perhaps at first this concept may seem abstract and confusing. After all, how can you play an instrument with your mind? What does this idea mean exactly? The answers to these perfectly reasonable questions are discussed below.

Obsessive Thinking

There are various forms of thinking. One form is agitated, obsessive thinking, which, instead of being a strategy for improving your musical study, becomes a huge obstacle to the healthy, creative development of your ability. This type of thinking can even block you mentally. This will affect your musical performance and your physical condition in various ways. This is why it is essential to understand the reasons for this all-too-common situation for artists, in order to find new directions that can help you achieve a fully realized, tension-free musical performance. You need to observe your own mental activity in order to become aware of your conscious and subconscious programming, so that you can reprogram your mind to embrace a free and expressive approach to your instrument.

As an example of the effect of obsessive thinking, imagine that you have a concert coming up in a few days. Merely thinking about it may in some cases make you feel nervous, putting thoughts in your mind like: "How am I going to handle playing in front of so many people?" or "what happens if I make a mistake in that difficult passage?" Why do you feel this way? Why do our stomachs churn merely by thinking about playing in public? Shouldn't you be happy to share your music with an audience? This is, after all, one of the aims of music. Nevertheless, the nerves continue, affecting your daily study, making it the exact opposite of the enjoyment that you could be experiencing when you play your instrument each day.

What causes these nerves? Are they caused by the prospect of performing a piece of music in public? It may indeed be that the idea of playing to an audience is what causes tension and nerves, as deep down lies a fear of making mistakes, of being judged, or feeling frustrated when performing in public.

This idea, which has nothing at all to do with the essence of the art of music, comes into existence in your mind. It totally affects your perspective of the concert and gives you a feeling of insecurity. The physical reality of the performance has not even arrived yet, but this mental terror is already projecting forward to the actual moment of the concert. In other words, you are anticipating the event mentally, but in a way that makes you feel physically blocked about it. Your body is experiencing this future experience in the present, but in a distorted way.

This situation is caused by obsessive thinking, which can paralyse you mentally, emotionally, and physically. This enactment of a future event is so powerful that the event itself may indeed unfold exactly as you'd imagined it. But you need to bear in mind that you have created it yourself with your way of thinking and feeling. It is a form of mental programming that you have established in relation to what the stage means for you. It is time to start changing that programming.

This kind of mental programming was something I faced with my teacher in Switzerland. The thought of playing in class had me trembling with nerves. As a result, my practice at home was pure torture. Now I realize that I anticipated the situation with my way of thinking and feeling in those days.

In the world of music this is a common situation for students and professionals alike. The level of anxiety may be higher or lower, depending on the individual. What is important is to analyze why such situations occur and to seek alternatives that will help you enjoy playing your instrument. Once you find those alternatives, you will experience a profound change. In time, that change will become more and more evident in a spectacular way, in your personal life and in your life as an artist. For me, this type of change is constant in my artistic and personal development. This is the beauty of music: that it helps us to grow day by day as human beings and as souls touched by the magic of the art.

Constructive Thinking

What would happen if you suddenly became aware that the problem described above is initially caused by a "mental" situation? What would you do about it? Would you continue with the same mental attitude, or would you start to transform your thinking into something healthy, caring, and creative? Can you imagine a daily music practice free of mental tensions, filled instead with creativity and love? Can you imagine enjoying the full experience of playing in front of an audience?

All this can happen if you allow yourself to discover your true mental potential and apply it in your daily music practice. If you do, you will start thinking in a more creative, deeper, and healthier way. For example, instead of thinking that performing in public scares you, try using your mental potential to transform that thought, which is holding you back, into a positive thought like the following, while at the same time holding an emotion of freedom and plenitude in your mind:

I FEEL GREAT WHEN I PLAY IN EVERY CONCERT THAT I GIVE. I EXPRESS MY MUSICAL IDEAS FREELY. I TRANSFORM THE HEARTS OF THE LISTENERS THROUGH THE POWER OF MUSIC.

This simple, healthy, and positive thought, in harmony with an elevated emotion, will even make your body feel a little more flexible and freer when playing both in your daily practice and at a musical event. Your body will be receiving clear instructions related to how it should feel in a public presentation. This is a powerful strategy, as by recognizing this fear of the stage, you can observe it, and in that moment, you can evoke a thought and emotion like those described above. This is a way of creating a new mental and physical approach to, in this case, your on-stage performance.

Of course, this is only one part of the mental transformation, but it forms the basis for building on the change. Transforming your image of yourself and of the world around you will give you the strength you need to explore this new approach to studying music. In this approach, your mind, emotions, and body must form a single unit. This will profoundly transform the way you play your instrument.

When applied to your daily practice, the power of this new way of thinking will have wonderful effects. I recall that on one occasion, one of my students, when he began to apply this approach, exclaimed with wonder: "it's like magic!" And indeed, a well-aimed word can create such magic, which simply means making use of the unlimited potential of your mental metacognitive capacities in all that you do. Moreover, behind this way of thinking lies the pure force of intention—the intention to feel fully present in your work as an artist.

The Effects of Thoughts on Playing Music

Perhaps while reading the above you were asking yourself: Does my way of thinking really influence my daily study? Is my way of thinking while practising really so important? What does this have to do with my performance as a musician?

In fact, there has been extensive scientific research into the powerful influence that our way of thinking has on our bodies. It has been found that negative thoughts and tension release stress hormones, like cortisol, causing physical exhaustion or fatigue. On the other hand, when our thoughts are creative and positive, the body produces chemical substances called endorphins and enkephalins, which promote physical and mental wellbeing.

With this in mind, one reason you should be careful with your thoughts when practising your instrument is the close relationship between your mind and your body, as you also play a musical instrument with "your instrument", i.e., your body.

To better understand this concept, try the following exercise:

1. Find a quiet place where you won't be interrupted.
2. Have your musical instrument on hand.
3. Choose a musical passage from a piece that you're studying.
4. Bring to your mind a stressful thought. For example: "I always mess up this part of the passage; it's too hard to play." Repeat it several times.
5. Take your instrument and play the passage.
6. When you're finished, stop and take note of how you felt physically and mentally while you were playing.
7. Now take three slow and deep abdominal breaths.
8. Bring to your mind a constructive thought, for example: "I know that I can play this passage very well and feel free while playing." Repeat this sentence (or another constructive sentence of your choice that enhances your relationship with the piece chosen for this exercise) several times.
9. Keep clear in your mind the direction of the music and the type of tone that you want to produce through this passage, like a mental sound map. Imagine yourself playing very well.
10. Perform the previous exercise again, but this time with your hands crossed over your heart, while at the same time conjuring an elevated emotion, like a feeling of plenitude.
11. Take your instrument and play the same musical passage.
12. Once again, note your perception of this last part of the exercise, i.e., how you felt physically and mentally while playing the passage.

Did you notice any difference between the two performances? How did your body and mind respond in the two different parts of the exercise? Was there any difference in your playing of the piece? Perhaps you noted only a minimal difference, or perhaps a huge one; the initial results vary from person to person. What is important here is to become aware of the effect your mind can have on your playing.

You may have noticed in the first part of the exercise that your muscles became stiff and prevented you from enjoying yourself while playing, while also hindering the natural flow of your creativity. Such thoughts might also have made you feel emotionally blocked, which can make your performance stilted, as if the mental tension were inhibiting the full expression of your true voice. These kinds of limiting and frustrating sensations are all too common for musicians; they are sensations that divert us from our real mission as artists.

During the second part of the exercise, you might have felt more flexibility in your muscles while playing, resulting in a better physical and mental state during your performance and a more natural and profound fluidity in the piece you were playing. Without a doubt your mental focus was better, making the energy of your playing more powerful than it was in the first part of the exercise.

What is most revealing is that your fear of making mistakes begins to vanish simply because you are channeling your mental energy creatively rather than destructively. When you tap into your mental metacognitive capacities, all fear will begin to vanish from the image you have of yourself and of playing music. You will be directing your energy towards the results that you really want to express in your musical performance.

In Exercise Nine, what you are doing is using a mental metacognitive capacity referred to in scientific discourse as visual motor rehearsal. This technique, which will be explained further below, involves mentally visualizing yourself performing a musical piece exactly as you want to play it. It is a technique that has been used by professional athletes and NASA astronauts for years.

Thus, with constant practice based on the elements of the second part of the exercise, you can develop your mental potential to improve the way you play a musical instrument. Through this new way of thinking and feeling, you will be able to play in a way that is genuine and free of both physical and mental obstacles.

In each part of the exercise, you will notice a difference in your emotional state. In the first, you may feel a sensation of frustration or fear. In the second, you may perceive a sense of confidence or wellbeing.

Both of these emotions will seriously affect how you play, because the feeling that arises from your thoughts will be the one you express in your performance. Recognizing this and knowing that you have the capacity to decide how you want to play music and how you want to feel while playing is already a big step forward.

Of course, you also need an excellent music teacher or guide who can help you develop an effective technique and expressive musicality. It is a question of teamwork, as it is extremely important to have the support of a good teacher with a creative and effective study method. However, the results of studying depend on you, because you will spend most of your time practising completely alone. You need to be aware that regardless of the guidance you receive, you have an excellent teacher inside you. It is this idea that will help you turn your study time from a mere routine into something truly creative and productive where you can apply your mental, emotional, and physical metacognitive skills effectively.

The Thought-Feeling-Action Relationship

All of the above suggests that the first step towards creating a new technical-musical foundation is to transform our thoughts about the world of sound and about ourselves. Every apparent problem must first be solved at the mental level, through creative thinking supported by a clear mental picture. Having a clear mental picture of how you want to play will give you a sense of confidence that will lead to the right physical actions to achieve your musical goal.

It is important not only to start using creative thoughts in your daily practice, but also to connect this new vision of the world of sound to nature, so that you won't forget where the essence of sound really comes from. If you are open to it, this essence will find a perfect medium of expression in you. This idea will be explored in more detail in the next chapter.

Scientific research has proven the impact that both negative and positive thoughts can have on our physical condition. The neuroscientific researcher Dr. Joe Dispenza (2007, p.43) offers a clear description of what happens to thoughts on a physiological level: "Your every thought produces a biochemical reaction in the brain. The brain then releases chemical signals that are transmitted to the body, where they act as the messengers of the thought. The thoughts that produce the chemicals in the brain allow your body to *feel* exactly the way you were just thinking." In other words, thoughts generate feelings and feelings generate thoughts in keeping with those feelings.

According to Garello (2016), when we have negative thoughts we also create negative emotions, and this makes our body generate cortisol, a hormone that over time can cause muscle pain and cramps. On the other hand, positive thoughts create positive emotions and the body generates serotonin or oxytocin, chemicals that relax our body.

When advanced music students play their instrument, feelings of stress are very common. This is why it is important to be aware of this phenomenon and find healthy and creative ways to apply your thoughts with a clear intention before you start playing.

The science on the physical effect of our thoughts confirms the importance of developing a new, musical metacognitive strategy for learning an instrument. The new strategy I propose is self-correction, which forms part of the teaching method described in this book. This strategy involves correcting yourself in the first person. For example, if your tuning was not quite right when playing a musical passage, visualize playing in your mind and support your visualization with a statement like, "My tuning is perfect in this musical passage." With this strategy, your mind will be focusing on what you want to improve, and your intention will be fully focused on that musical element exactly as you have mentally planned it. Your ear will also know exactly what it wants to hear. It is important to detect faults, but even more important to orient your mind towards the solutions, not the mistakes.

Self-correction is also an excellent strategy for overcoming stage fright. For example, instead of feeding fear over a future public performance with thoughts like, "I know I'm not going to play well," or "I'm terrified of making a mistake," like the examples from the study of stage fright in Spain, try focusing on creative thoughts like, "I feel very good playing in the concert," or "my playing is brilliant and expressive." It is very important to express your self-correction statements in the present tense as if what you're expressing is already a reality; and when you speak them, make an effort to feel them fully.

Behind every self-correction lies a clear and precise intention related to how you want to play your musical instrument. It is essential in this process to really believe in your self-corrections, as only then will they have an effect on your playing.

As the Austrian philosopher Rudolf Steiner once said: "Man knows that only by allowing himself to be guided by 'upright thoughts' both in his cognition and in his acts can he fulfil his mission" (Steiner, 1996, p.27).

What Steiner proposes is that by vesting our thoughts with warmth, love, and creativity, we can realize our true potential as human beings to the fullest. This is why our minds are co-creators of music, because music finds its full expression, its perfection, in human beings. With this in mind, we need to learn how to emanate music through our instrument in the most faithful and expressive way possible. One way to achieve this is to use and unite our mental, emotional, and physical metacognitive capacities to the utmost.

In the following section, I will discuss a mental metacognitive strategy that is central to the Conscious Musician method: visual motor rehearsal.

Visual Motor Rehearsal and its Effects on Playing Music

> If you have been there in the mind, you'll go there in the body. (Waitley, quoted by Dayton, 2013, p 282)

Visual motor rehearsal was introduced at NASA and to the US Olympic team by its creator, Denis Waitley, in 1984. This technique, which involves mentally visualizing a specific routine prior to its physical execution, has been found to have an extraordinary effect on the results of the routine when it is actually performed. In an experiment directed by Waitley, athletes were hooked up to a biofeedback machine while they visualized their routine. The results were astounding, as it was found that the athletes' neuronal transmission sequences were the same for their visualization as they were for the physical activity of the routine itself. If athletes can obtain great results from visual motor rehearsals, musicians can also enhance their playing by implementing this technique in their daily practice.

Dispenza suggests that "powerful changes take place in brain activity and in our perceptions when we lock in our focused concentration. We lose track of time and space. Most significantly, our body grows quiet, and we enter a trance-like state" (Dispenza, 2007, p.393). This describes the visualization process exactly. Once your body tunes into your profound mental state of concentration, you will be able to see how you really want to play your instrument. That is when the true changes in your playing will begin to take place.

When you achieve a profound level of concentration, your brainwaves shift from beta (alert) state to alpha (creative) state. When your brain is in an alpha state, your visualization will be more effective, because it is in this state that your conscious mind connects with your unconscious mind, while your analytical mind keeps quiet. Your mind's orders will be communicated directly to your body. Your musical ideas will be expressed freely in your musical performance.

Various scientific experiments have been conducted to examine what happens on the neuronal level when we use mental visualization. In his book *The Brain that Changes Itself*, Norman Doidge (2007) describes one of these experiments carried out by Alvaro Pascual-Leone, professor of neuroscience at Harvard Medical School. The experiment involved teaching a sequence of notes on piano to two groups of people who had never played this instrument before. The first group carried out a mental rehearsal while sitting for two hours every day for five days, imagining playing the melody on the piano. The second group practised the same sequence physically on a piano for the same amount of time every day. The two groups were hooked up to a computer to record their neural activity while they carried out the mental or physical practice.

Pascual-Leone found that the two groups experienced similar changes to their brain map. The mental practice had produced the same physiological changes as the physical practice. At the end of the experiment the group that had practised physically played the piece better. However, after the mental practice group were allowed two hours of physical practice, it was found that they played the piece better than the group that had only practised the passage physically. This is a clear example of the important role that mental rehearsal can play in the development of musical ability, and that every technical or musical problem is resolved first on the mental level. If you think of your mind as your best ally for developing your skills as a musician, you can use its power to achieve the full expression of your true talents.

Visual motor rehearsal is a key part of the teaching strategies in the Conscious Musician method for everyday practice, and it is also an excellent way of preparing for a concert. This teaching strategy is so powerful that even visualizing a public performance in a place where you have not been physically present will give you the sensation that you have already performed there when you arrive at the venue on the day of the event.

The second part of this book includes specific exercises for studying an instrument and performing on stage, comprising mental metacognitive elements based on visual motor rehearsal to help overcome musical and technical challenges in your daily music practice.

For now, I invite you to try the following activities to begin internalizing this principle as part of your daily study:

1. Lie down on a yoga mat. Ensure that your neck and head are aligned.
2. Inhale in this position for four beats, hold your breath for one beat, and exhale for four beats. Repeat this sequence five times.
3. Once you are breathing steadily and deeply, cross your hands over the middle of your chest. Breathe from your diaphragm, inhaling for four beats, holding your breath for two, and exhaling for another four.
4. Maintain the position of step three and visualize yourself playing an extract of a piece you are studying. Make your visualization as detailed as possible. Imagine the sound, your technical level, your phrasing, and how you want to feel while playing. Perform this step three times.
5. Play the extract with your musical instrument.

At the end of these activities, write down your reflections and observations. The results will vary from person to person. For the visual motor rehearsal to have a really powerful effect on your music practice, it must be repeated constantly.

When you start applying this strategy in your practice, you can do it in one of two ways. The first is to observe yourself from the perspective of the audience, seeing yourself as you want to play. In other words, seeing yourself from outside. The second is to visualize your performance from your perspective as the musician; in other words, looking from yourself outwards.

A very important element of this strategy is the mental sound map. This teaching strategy, which forms part of the Conscious Musician method, is explained below.

Mental Sound Map

By now it will have become obvious why it is important to use visual motor rehearsal in your daily music practice just as it has been used by athletes for years. An important element in this visualization process while practising is the mental sound map.

In the world of acoustics, sound mapping is a technique that helps to identify the sonority of an area, neighbourhood, or city. It can show us what a busy street, an open space, or a downtown area can sound like (Prieto, 2016).

Just as this technique can reveal the sonority of a geographical area, the mental sound map for a piece of music can express it in your mind in a very precise way. Just as an architect makes drawings of her work before it gets built, musicians can make a mental sound map of the pieces they are going to play. Based on this clear and concise map, you can begin to plot the pathway towards playing exactly as you have imagined it in your mind.

This map consists of having a clear idea in your mind of the sound, the musical intentions, the dynamics, the phrasing, the transitions, and the breaths. This will turn your hearing into your best teacher, because you will know what you want to hear at each moment. Moreover, by knowing what you want to hear, you will know what you want to improve when you repeat a passage, which will transform your repetitions from mechanical routines into conscious, creative exercises.

Using a mental sound map is like seeing a piece of music "from above" in a holistic, global way. The more precise your mental map is, the greater will be your ability to play the way you want to in your musical performances. It is like an eagle's flight high in the sky, where it can see all the wonders of the natural world. It is through the power of thought that you can access your true potential as an artist of sound and become a messenger of the magic of music with every note you play.

The next section deals with a key element of the didactic principles explored in this book: the musician's emotions and the power of a harmonious heart when playing an instrument.

1.4. EMOTIONAL AWARENESS IN THE WORLD OF SOUND

> Every one of us has a door into our emotions. It is up to each of us to chose to keep it closed or to allow the key in our minds to open it so that our emotions may be expressed in our actions totally and fully. (Anonymous)

Playing with Feeling

In your life as a musician you have likely often heard the idea that the most important thing in playing music is to play with feeling, to express ourselves through the music. And you have likely thought and experienced this idea many times. Or perhaps something like the following has happened to you, too. During my studies in Switzerland, it was common for students to ask each other to listen to a piece they were practising before their class. One day, one of my fellow students asked me if I could listen to how she played a certain piece. Her performance of the piece was technically quite good, but somewhat stilted. When she finished playing, I suggested that perhaps she should keep a specific emotion in her mind so that she could make her playing more expressive. She replied: "No way! I have to concentrate totally on my fingers because when I feel excited, I lose control of the piece."

This imbalance between body and emotions is something that often happens in the music world. It is as if our minds were cordoned off on one side and our emotions on the other. The problem is that being "excited when we play" is not enough to achieve a truly expressive performance. And concentrating only on the physical aspect of our performance, like my fellow student was doing, is unlikely to result in a moving interpretation of the piece. Therefore, it is necessary to know exactly what kind of emotion you want to convey to be able to express it consciously and naturally through your body, hence the importance of developing an emotional awareness within the world of sound. And more important still is the need to make contact with the wisdom of your heart and to create heart coherence so that your emotions can flow in all their splendour when you play your instrument. A harmonious heart will generate a coherent mind that will enable you to find effective, creative solutions in the process of studying your musical instrument.

The most memorable aspect of any musical performance is the emotion that it inspires both in the musician and in the audience. Indeed, as noted above, what is most important is to play with feeling, as this is what will give vibrancy to your performance, and it is precisely this vibrancy that will reach the heart of the listener and spark a transformation. This is, of course, one of the missions of music. This is why the musical presentations of the future should be focused on bringing the hearts of the audience into coherence. The third part of this book discusses this type of concert in detail.

We know from our own experience that an essential part of the world of sound consists in that flurry of emotions that it produces in us when we listen to it attentively. For example, listening to Rossini's *Barber of Seville* may give you a sensation of joy or lightness, while listening to Vivaldi's "Winter" may produce a feeling of peace. And if you give all your attention to a Bach cantata, you may experience an emotion so pure that it gives you a sense of the divine character of the music within you. It is as if one of the functions of music were to elicit pure, uplifting emotions from the mind, elevating our souls and uniting us with the mystical dimension of the world of sound.

Moreover, the same piece of music may evoke different feelings, ranging from sorrow to joy or excitement. This is certainly what happens with Mahler's Fifth Symphony, whose second movement is dominated by a feeling of furious rage, which is transformed into a sense of triumph and delight in the last movement. It would be possible to list countless examples of musical works that highlight the intimate relationship between our emotions and the world of music, but for now it is enough simply to be aware of this relationship and find ways of manifesting it.

But what does it mean to play with feeling? What does "being expressive" refer to exactly?

Perhaps the first thing that comes to your mind is that you need to use more vibrato, play more loudly, or be more confident when you play. All these ideas are perfectly valid. Of course, we need these and other elements to make our playing more expressive. But these elements are largely physical. Indeed, we invariably focus our attention on how we can be more expressive by using physical techniques, when instead we should be focusing first on the type of emotion that we want to feel and emanate. This, in time, will guide us naturally to the physical movements needed to achieve an emotive performance that is profound and vibrant.

Consider the following situation. You see a *pianissimo* written on the sheet music for the piece you are practising. Instead of thinking that you need to play with less force, think of an emotion, for example, a sensation of mystery. Experiencing this emotion within will lead to movements that correspond naturally to the *pianissimo* and at the same time create a sensation of magic. This magic and beauty in music is what we always need to look for within us, both in our daily practice and in every musical event. It is essential to experience and feel each specific emotion that we want to express through our sonic art so that the emotion is authentic and can reach the innermost fibres of the being of the listener.

The Fear of Making a Mistake

> This obsession with mistakes and correcting them will thus become, whether we want it to or not, one of the pillars of action among teachers and students, where the learner will always be worried about mistakes and will experience music in terms of this fear of error. (Pozo, 2020)

The impact of the emotions on the body is something that has been scientifically proven. An emotion like fear, which can release high levels of cortisol, will provoke tension in your body, while happiness, which can release the love hormone known as oxytocin, will lead to a state of relaxation and contentment.

Goleman (2005) describes what happens on the physiological level when we experience different emotions:

> With fear, blood goes to the large skeletal muscles, causing the body to freeze. Circuits in the brain's emotional centers trigger a flood of hormones that put the body on general alert. With happiness there is an increased activity in a brain center that inhibits negative feelings and increases available energy. This configuration offers the body a general rest, as well as enthusiasm for whatever task is at hand and for striving toward a great variety of goals. With love, a parasympathetic pattern arises that allows the body to feel calm and contentment. (Goleman, 2005, p.5-6)

Fear, whose physiological effects are described in the above quotation, has been a central part of learning a musical instrument for many students. For example, the phenomenon of being "afraid to make a mistake" when practising a musical instrument has existed for a long time within the classical music tradition. It is something that has been planted in students' subconscious minds for many years. Indeed, it is a fear that both students and teachers tend to share.

One of the reasons for this phenomenon is the popular expectation in music teaching that students should play every piece perfectly exactly as it is written. And if they make a mistake, it is always serious. This idea really needs to change. If you are afraid of mistakes, you will be making music in a space of insecurity. In his master classes, Benjamin Zanders, the conductor of the Boston Youth Symphony, guides his students to react positively to any challenge they face. He tells them that such challenges are an opportunity for improvement. This attitude alone will already facilitate a much healthier approach to the process of learning a musical instrument. Students will be able to create out of love, not out of fear.

In any case, not knowing exactly what you want to express in a performance can have repercussions that are not only mental but physical as well, as your body will respond in a tense and rigid way to a lack of emotional certainty. On the other hand, if you make contact with the creative centre of your heart and are aware of the kind of feelings you want to express, your body will react more naturally and freely, as the emotions-body connection is as intimate as the mind-body connection. In short, a particular thought produces a particular feeling, which in turn produces a particular action.

> What emotions could be expressed by a terrified student, who has no trust in their own musical skills? (Pozo, 2020)

The above quotation perfectly expresses what happened to me in my time studying at the Conservatory. When my first teacher in Switzerland urged me repeatedly to play with more expression, his intention no doubt was to improve the expressive quality of my playing. But it isn't enough to tell a student to "play with more expression" without explaining what this means. The only thing it achieved in my case was to increase my physical tension, because I was exerting myself physically unnecessarily in an effort to compensate somehow for a lack of expression.

As soon as I realized that every problem needs to be resolved first in my mind, I discovered that I also had to experience and consciously feel the full range of emotions transmitted through the sound itself to be able to turn my playing into an event full of captivating magic. Some time has passed since then and I have found that the stronger I can personally experience an emotion, the greater the impact it will have on the sound that emanates from the depths of my being. The road is endless, as is the power of sound.

Perhaps at this point you're wondering what happens if you don't know exactly what you want to express. Why do you have to be conscious of your emotions when you play? Why do your emotions affect your physical state during your performance?

Here's an example that could answer these questions and illustrate the importance of our emotions as an infallible means of expressing the music truly and fully: imagine that you have just five minutes left until your exam or a concert you are playing in. You know that a lot of people will be listening to you. This might make you uncomfortable, and you start feeling butterflies in your stomach and your body starts to shudder. When you walk out on stage and start to play you feel a physical turmoil that greatly influences your performance. Instead of enjoying it, it becomes a kind of torture, and it is this emotional energy that you end up conveying to the audience.

All this tension in your performance arose from an emotion: anxiety, which can release chemicals in your body like cortisol. This emotion was created out of the fear of making a mistake in front of so many people and feeling frustrated with yourself as a musician and as a person. This situation is common to both students and professionals.

The problem behind this situation is that you are stepping out onto the stage with an imbalanced heart caused by the emotion of fear. This emotion causes a trembling sensation in the stomach that will automatically have a negative impact on your whole body, which in some cases can result in a loss of physical control.

To deal with situations like the one described above, you need to establish a conscious emotional bridge between yourself and the music you're playing. Discovering this bridge will open up a new experience for you as an artist of sound. In the second part of this book, specific exercises are described to help strengthen this bridge and develop your emotional metacognitive potential as a musician, in addition to achieving heart coherence, which is the basis on which your true emotions can be expressed through your music.

The Power of Images

> Art reveals the hidden powers of Nature, which finds in Man its full expression, its perfection. (Anonymous)

An effective way of becoming consciously expressive and establishing a balance between mind, emotions, and body is by maintaining a mental image while you're playing. This image may be an element of nature that inspires a specific emotion or sensation in you. This point, so crucial to changing your vision and interpretation of music, will be discussed in further detail in the following chapters. For now, I would like to invite you to try the following two-part exercise to give you a clearer idea of the topic of this chapter.

Exercise Part One:

1. Find a quiet place to study.
2. Play a passage of the piece you are currently studying.
3. Try to play that passage as expressively as possible several times.
4. Take a break.
5. Write down your reflections on how you felt physically and emotionally while playing and some of the thoughts that passed through your mind while performing the passage.

You may have found that despite your intention to play as expressively as possible, you didn't experience a satisfying result because you didn't have a clear idea of the kind of emotion (e.g., melancholy, joy, courage) that you were trying to emanate through your music. This can cause physical tension, as not having a clear idea of the specific emotion you're seeking will result in straining body movements intended to "be expressive" in response to your intention to express yourself while playing. This can even cause a certain distortion in the sound and close the door on your emotions altogether. This blockage is the cause of expressive tension arising from emotional uncertainty.

Exercise Part Two: Before completing the second part of the exercise, take a few long, deep abdominal breaths. You can do this sitting or lying down. The important thing is to have your back as straight as possible and relax your mind and body through breathing before continuing. Take the time you need to achieve a state of complete relaxation. Then go on to the next steps.

1. Imagine, in as much detail as possible, an element of nature that is related to the same musical passage selected for part one of the exercise.
2. Allow this image to provoke a series of emotions in you. Feel these emotions inside you as deeply as you can. Feel how your heart relaxes and emanates an energy from within.
3. Choose the specific emotion that you feel the greatest affinity for and that you believe has the strongest connection to the musical passage. Allow your heart to feel this emotion as deeply as possible.
4. Imagine the sound and musical direction (i.e., the phrasing) that you want to give this part of your piece while holding onto the emotion you wish to emanate while playing. Place your hands over your heart during this step.
5. Pick up your instrument. Imagine once more the element of nature you chose. Feel the emotion that this incites in you once again.
6. Take a deep breath and play the passage again, observing your concentration, emotions, and physical state as you play. If possible, play with your eyes closed, keeping the image of nature present in your mind.
7. Repeat points one to six two or three times.
8. When finished, write down your reflections and observations in your notebook.

The power of the image is very strong. It can help you achieve true concentration because you are focusing on an element on the mental level, which in turn unleashes your creativity. The image also automatically inspires a specific feeling in you, which you can express consciously through your instrument.

By holding onto an image of nature while playing, your analytical mind takes a back seat and coherence is established between your conscious mind (the part of your mind that stores explicit memories) and your subconscious mind (where implicit memories are stored). The physical effect of this coherence is the release of endorphins in your body, which facilitates a better physical, emotional, and mental performance.

It is worth highlighting the point that the relationship between nature and music has been an important consideration in the world of composition throughout music history. Composers like Vivaldi, Brahms, Beethoven, and Messiaen took inspiration from nature to create their masterpieces. For Beethoven, nature was a refuge as well as an inspiration. He would spend hours walking in the forest. In one of his notebooks, he wrote: "My decree is to remain in the country [...] It is as if every tree in the country spoke to me: "Holy! Holy! Ecstasy in the woods! Sweet stillness! Let the wind not hold me in Vienna!" (Santacecilia, 2013).

Another element that can be extremely helpful for your emotional metacognitive development as a musician is to be constantly asking yourself whether your heart is really open and whether you are feeling the emotion you are seeking when playing. This will take the creative process of playing a piece of music to a more profound and powerful level.

The Effects of Conscious Feeling

All of this has a very positive effect on your physical state when you play. By being guided by your mind and emotions, your body will feel freer and more flexible when playing. For example, imagining a mountain can give you a feeling of strength and magnitude, which in turn will elicit the appropriate movement from your body to express the sound corresponding to that image. This will awaken the latent bond between mind, emotions, and body, a bond that will make you one with the world of sound.

This way of seeing and studying a musical instrument will also sharpen your listening and observation, thereby enhancing the technical and expressive quality of your daily practice, and the enjoyment of that practice, which will be reflected naturally in your playing before an audience. Your mind and emotions are the perfect guide for your physical and internal hearing, and for finding the physical movements that can faithfully and naturally represent your artistic intentions.

Of course, if you have never tried these kinds of exercises before in your practice, have patience! In the beginning the effects may not be so noticeable. But if you can persevere and have faith in your true expressive abilities and in the creative process, you will achieve great results. You will also turn each practice with your instrument into a work of art, as you will be bringing your whole self to it: your mind, your emotions, and your body. It is a new way of seeing and studying music. If you are open to it, this approach will enrich your path through the magnificent and magical world of sound. You will realize that "being expressive" means bringing to life within you the latent need to experience, feel, and know the exact kind of emotion or emotions that you want to convey through the music.

> ...The highest feelings are, as a matter of fact, not those which come 'of themselves', but those which are achieved by energetic and persevering work in the realm of thought... (Steiner, 1996 p. 28)

Technique as a Need for Expression

I recently had a conversation with an advanced student that I have been working with for the past two years. She told me that she studied technique for hours and hours with one of her previous teachers but never achieved the level that the teacher expected of her. And moreover, she studied in constant fear of not achieving her goals. Working with the methods of the Conscious Musician has helped her to understand technique in a completely different way, not as a mechanical element, but as a need for pure and convincing expression. In other words, every physical movement in her playing comes from the depths of her heart and from an intention to create beauty through the world of sound.

The history behind musical technique is worth reflecting on here. Methods in technique have been applied since the eighteenth century and have come to form an extremely important part of the process of learning a musical instrument. As described by Javier Duque (2013), the revolutionary model in music teaching was founded on the coordination of teachers and curriculum designers to develop methods that provide the most objective corpus of musical knowledge possible to create a standard set of topics to be taught; in other words, a scientific perspective was adopted as the basis of music methodology.

Since that era, the technique has been taught separately from the performance of musical pieces. This is very much a feature of curricula at schools of music today. Students are expected to develop their skills on both the technical and the musical levels. This split perception can sometimes create physical tensions in students. Changing this perception is therefore essential for the healthy, creative development of a student's proficiency with an instrument.

The view of technique as a mere mechanical movement that helps students master their instrument needs to be abandoned. Instead, technique should be viewed as a need for expression. An extremely important part of this is understanding a healthy body as the foundation for an expressive musical performance. In this way, "technique" will be transformed from a mere mechanical component to a pursuit of the finest musical expression and a powerful use of the body to achieve it. The application of the teaching principles of the Conscious Musician can establish this connection between technique and musicality, viewing both elements as means of expression in playing an instrument. This perspective is equally applicable to any playing method.

Heart Intelligence

All the concepts considered in this chapter point to the conclusion that within your heart lies an extraordinary power of expression. But to access that power, you need to be in tune with your heart.

It is essential to establish heart coherence before experiencing the emotions you want to emanate. Those emotions will be even more powerful because your physical performance will find the perfect way of expressing them. An activity for establishing heart coherence is offered below.

The stress of playing in public, for example, creates heart incoherence, and this in turn creates incoherence in your mind because your heart sends information instantly to your brain. This is why developing heart coherence is essential not only to achieve an authentic expression but also to achieve a high level of playing. As discussed in the third part of this book, it also opens up a new way of performing concerts where the music is not merely entertainment but an event where both artist and audience can be transformed by the music.

It is clear from the above that establishing a healthy relationship with your emotions is vitally important. This emotional connection creates an electromagnetic field around you that will influence your playing in an extraordinary way.

The concept of heart coherence was developed by the HeartMath Institute (HeartMath is a registered trademark of Quantum Intech, Inc. For all HeartMath trademarks go to www.heartmath.com/trademarks). By applying a few simple techniques, you can connect to your emotional intelligence and establish heart coherence that transforms the way you play. These techniques are outlined further below.

Heart coherence is the main focus of the HeartMath Institute, a non-profit organization founded in Boulder Creek, Colorado in 1991 (Childre and Martin, 1999, quoted by Edwards, S., Edwards, D. 2018, p. 2). This institute has carried out extensive research on the benefits of developing heart coherence on both personal and social levels.

> In pursuit of a central vision and mission to facilitate personal, social, and global coherence, the institute has pioneered integral, heart-focused research in neuroscience, cardiology, physiology, biochemistry, bioelectricity, physics, and psychology. This research has enabled the development of practical, heart-based strategies and biofeedback technology (Childre et al. 2016) to facilitate heart rate variability (HRV) and psychophysiological coherence and positive emotions such as peace and appreciation. (Edwards & Edwards, 2018)

A few months ago, I had a revealing experience with one of my students. It was just when I had begun using techniques to establish heart coherence in my music teaching.

In a group session, each student was asked to cross their hands over the middle of their hearts while listening to their fellow students playing. At the end of each piece, I asked one of the students listening and the student who had played the piece to express what they felt. After the last student took his turn and I asked him how he had felt playing, I was amazed by his response: "I felt my depression leave my body, and I was filled with a happiness that I can't explain." By opening his heart, he had allowed the power of the music to cure his emotional state in that moment.

This prompted me to reflect on how establishing heart coherence while listening to or playing a musical instrument can turn classical music into a healing experience. By being in harmony with your heart, you allow the true meaning of the world of sound to take effect, elevating your spirit in an extraordinary way. And establishing heart coherence can have a powerful impact on your musical performance. When you place your attention on the centre of your heart, your body will begin to react much more naturally, becoming a unique and wondrous medium of expression. This is something that I have experienced time and again with my own playing and with my students. At the neuronal level, by placing your attention on the centre of your heart, your brainwaves shift from beta (alert state) to alpha (relaxed and creative state).

To be able to connect to the heart of a piece of music, you first need to establish a profound connection with your emotional state and find a state of emotional coherence. Only in this way will you be able to build a bridge between yourself and the music.

Before carrying out activities to develop a coherent heart, try the following exercises of the Quick Coherence* technique:[1]

Step 1. Focus your attention on the area of the heart. Imagine your breath is flowing in and out of your heart or chest area, breathing a little slower and deeper than usual. Find an easy rhythm that is comfortable.

Step 2. As you continue heart-focused breathing, make a sincere attempt to experience a regenerative feeling such as appreciation or care for someone or something in your life.

---

1 The Quick Coherence* technique to establish heart coherence is recommended by the HeartMath Institute (HeartMath is a registered trademark of Quantum Intech, Inc. For all HeartMath trademarks go to www.heartmath.com/trademarks).

Completing these simple steps will make your heart more harmonious, shifting your brainwaves from beta to alpha and making your playing more coherent and creative. This will create an emotional foundation for the development of your expressiveness when playing your musical instrument.

Next, try the following exercises to begin applying this principle in your daily practice:

1. Choose a piece of music to listen to.
2. Lie down on a yoga mat or something similar. Ensure that your neck is in line with your spine.
3. Breathe deeply, inhaling for four beats and exhaling for another four beats. Continue breathing deeply until you feel completely relaxed.
4. Cross your hands over the centre of your chest and perform the Quick Coherence® technique while listening to the piece of music you have chosen.
5. Sit up again and write down your reflections.
6. Choose a passage from a piece that you are currently studying.
7. With attention on the centre of your heart, complete a mental sound map of the piece.
8. Stand in a playing position and breathe slowly and deeply.
9. While playing, place all your attention on the centre of your heart (central area of the chest).
10. Take a break.
11. Play the same passage again, placing your attention on the centre of your heart and feeling a specific emotion while playing.
12. Write down your reflections.

The activities outlined above constitute an essential basis for the development of a musician's emotional dimension. By creating a coherent heart, you will be laying a solid foundation for your emotional metacognitive capacities in relation to your musical creativity. This question will be explored further in the second and third parts of this book.

Playing from the Heart

A student from Spain, a member of my Wednesday Sonata and Leader Class at the New England Conservatory, asked me to coach him in preparation for an audition for the position of associate principal cellist of the Barcelona Symphony Orchestra. He played his pieces through with elegance and accuracy. It was playing of a professional standard, the kind of performance that would, I told him, gain him entry into the ranks of an orchestra. However, it lacked flair and the characteristics of true leadership; not only command of colour, intensity, drive, and passion but the energy to take people beyond where they would normally go. We started work on the pieces; I played the piano, sang, coaxed, and urged him on until his rather formal restraint broke down, and he began to play from the heart and throw all his passion and energy into the soaring passages of the Dvorak Concerto. In the middle of his most impassioned utterances, I stopped him and said "There, that's it. If you play that way, they will not be able to resist you. You will be a compelling force behind which everyone will be inspired to play their best. (Zander & Zander, 2000)

Benjamin Zander, Conductor of the Boston Philharmonic, does extraordinary work in his group classes for players of different musical instruments. What has struck me most about his work, that which makes him stand out from other teachers of specific instruments, is how he is able to transform the way the participants play through an emotional change in their relationship with their playing. Zander opens their hearts to the possibility of a transformation on the stage, where they can emanate a captivating energy to their listening audience. The level of heart coherence and relaxation they achieve enables them to tap into their true expressive potential.

This is why I believe in the importance of establishing heart coherence, of identifying and experiencing every expression you want to convey and allowing this to guide you to find the right physical actions to faithfully represent both your musical ideas and the captivating energy of your emotional world. Because a musician is a creator of sound, a musical actor on the stage, and a musical artistic dancer.

1.5. THE TEMPERAMENTS IN THE WORLD OF MUSIC

One Man's Meat...

Have you ever wondered why you identify more with some pieces of music than others? Wondering about this fact is exactly what led me to ponder the phenomenon of temperaments as it applies to the world of music.

There are pieces that we enjoy studying more. It is as if they touch a part of us more deeply than others. Some pieces may provoke a feeling of sadness or melancholy in us, while others may fill us with energy or happiness. This is because the piece itself contains a kind of prevailing character, which is related to our own or with which we feel an affinity. It is thus very common to hear of musicians who are better at playing certain works than others, and so become "specialists" in a specific composer or musical genre. A great example of this is Glenn Gould (1932-1982), the Canadian pianist who came to be considered an expert in the works of the German composer J. S. Bach. It is important to identify this relationship between you and music, as it will be extremely helpful in guiding the development of your relationship between yourself and the art of sound.

The Four Temperaments

The concept of the four temperaments refers to a set of characteristics that describe the relationship between a person's inner world and the outer world. The predominance of one of these four over the others produces an essential aspect of the human personality, commonly known as the "temperament". The four-temperament model is a way of describing the character of humans in relation to the world around them. From ancient times until the Middle Ages, philosophers used their understanding of the four temperaments to explain personality differences between individuals.

The theory of the temperaments is based on the teachings of Empedocles, a Greek philosopher who lived from 495 to 425 B.C. These teachings were derived from the four basic elements of Greek cosmology: earth, water, fire, and air. Later, Hippocrates expanded Empedocles's theory by relating the four elements to four *humours* (or bodily fluids). He believed that everybody had a mixture of humours but that there was one that generally predominated. Centuries later, the physician Galen of Pergamon further developed Hippocrates's ideas, associating the physiological characteristics of individuals with their emotional behaviour. He used this information to cure his patients. These ideas were introduced to educational theory in the early twentieth century by the German philosopher

Rudolf Steiner, who based some of his pedagogical ideas on the concept of the four temperaments.

The temperaments are: *melancholic, phlegmatic, sanguine,* and *choleric.* The melancholic temperament is characterized by a sense of tragedy and tends to be contemplative and introverted. It is associated with the earth element, which gives it a quality of heaviness. The phlegmatic temperament is relaxed and quiet and tends to seek out comfort. It is associated with water, which links it to a sense of fluidity. The sanguine temperament is lively and quick to change its mind. It is associated with air, which gives it a quality of lightness. The choleric temperament is characterized by decisiveness and determination. It is associated with fire due to its violently energetic nature.

Table 1: Descriptions of the Four Temperaments

TEMPERAMENT	ELEMENT	CHARACTERISTICS
CHOLERIC	FIRE	Energetic, impetuous, confident
SANGUINE	AIR	Light, creative, distracted
MELANCHOLIC	EARTH	Contemplative, introverted, gloomy
PHLEGMATIC	WATER	Flexible, laid-back, relaxed

Which of the temperaments do you identify with? Which one do you feel more of an affinity with? Reflect for a moment and determine which temperament describes you best. Generally speaking, we all have two temperaments clearly reflected in our personalities, although there is usually one that predominates.

This can also be true of a piece of music. For example, if we listen attentively to Vivaldi's "Summer", we may observe a choleric temperament in both the first and third movements, while in the second, a melancholic feeling prevails. Different temperaments may also be interwoven in a single movement, but with one inevitably prevailing, as is the case of the first movement of Brahms's Violin Concerto, in which a forceful, choleric character predominates, but with phlegmatic and melancholic turns at certain points in the piece. This perspective merely offers a rough guide for the development of our emotional awareness in relation with the world of music. Take some time to work out and experience and your own view of the temperaments of different musical works.

The Temperaments and the World of Music

Considering music in this way will lead you to marvel at the power and magnitude of the art form and how it can touch the most intimate fibres of our being. The more open we are to exploring the world of music and the full range of feelings and sensations that it can inspire in us, the more moving and extraordinary our work will be as performers. An awareness of the different temperaments offers another great way of identifying the profound emotional relationship we all have with music. It could be said that it is precisely this relationship that causes that special vibration that we feel when we are in full contact with the world of sound.

To experience this more clearly, try the following exercise.

1. Choose one of your favourite pieces of music.
2. Find a quiet place where you can listen to it. Adopt a position with your back straight and relaxed.
3. Take a few abdominal breaths to relax your mind and body.
4. Listen attentively to the piece, without any intention of analyzing it, but with a desire to experience the different emotions and sensations that it inspires within you. You may place your attention in the area of your heart while listening to the piece.
5. Try to feel the different temperaments that arise as you listen and to perceive how they influence your emotional state.
6. At the end of the exercise, describe your experience in your notebook (i.e., the kind of emotions or the temperaments that you felt while listening).

The exercise you have just completed is an excellent way of seeing and feeling music as a source of relaxation. This is because you have prepared yourself to listen to it in a different way, a way that creates a direct bridge between the music and you. You have allowed yourself to truly feel the power of the music within you, leaving aside any apparent musical/technical concerns or the habitual desire to analyze any work of music. This is an essential step towards a new way of understanding the art of sound, as for our performances to be authentic and moving we need to activate the latent bridge between ourselves and music. You need to develop the need to feel the full power of the music in your whole being. This feeling will help us better understand the sonic, rhythmic, and dynamic structure of works of music.

It is a good idea to try the exercise suggested above several times, using works by different composers and in different styles. This will help you consciously develop your sensibility and will greatly enrich your experience in playing music as you will be expressing yourself, through your instrument, more naturally and convincingly. It will also lead toward the development of an awareness that can help you experience and identify the specific emotions that you want to convey. Achieving this form of emotional musical consciousness will drastically change the way you play both in technical and in musical terms.

Finally, it is worth highlighting the relationship between the four temperaments and the four elements. As mentioned above, the choleric is related to fire, the melancholic to earth, the sanguine to air, and the phlegmatic to water. Considering this relationship can help in the identification of precise images of nature when playing a musical piece— images that evoke a particular temperament, since, as we already know, a thought corresponds to a feeling, which in turn corresponds to a particular action.

The intention of this chapter is to provoke further reflection on the importance of opening your emotions by using the powerful key that is found in your mind. Only in this way can your amazing and creative ideas be realized in an effective and powerful way through your primordial technique: your physical fitness. Every emotion truly felt will act as a bridge between mind and body. Allow yourself to experience the mysterious corners of your emotional being and let this sing through your musical instrument in a way that will resonate in every aspect of your life.

1.6. BODY AWARENESS IN MUSIC

Many musicians tend to round the shoulders, hunch the back, or lift one shoulder, creating a curve in the spine when they play. If you keep practising your instrument with these positions hour after hour, day after day, year after year, you may wind up with back or neck problems. If you are aware of being in these positions, you can counteract them by becoming more aware of how you carry or play your instrument. Therefore, to build a strong body for your instrument, it is necessary to start with building your foundation, which is good posture and proper body alignment. (Olsen, 2009, p.41)

The Body: Your Physical Condition as the Foundation for Playing Freely

Have you ever wondered what you play your musical instrument with? Perhaps when you reflect on this question, the first thing that comes to your mind is that you play with your body. But what part of your body do you play your musical instrument with? Do you think it is important to keep physically fit? Do you believe that your physical condition can influence your playing?

There is wisdom in your body that is waiting to be heard, so that your body itself can become the perfect instrument for expressing your musical ideas. Your body's condition is the foundation for playing freely and enjoyably.

Just as you have reflected on the importance of becoming aware of your mind and emotions when playing, it is also very important to observe your body both outside and during your daily practice. Your body language is a reflection of your inner state of mind. How you perceive your body is a key element of the new vision of music described in this book. The more aware you are of your physical presence and the more sensitive you become to your natural wellbeing, the more effective will be your physical actions when performing. You will begin to develop a new, healthier sensitivity to your body while you play.

It is very common for music students and professionals to suffer from muscle pains caused, in part, by the way they play their instruments and their habits when practising. In some cases, they may pay attention to these signals sent by their bodies, but in other cases they may simply ignore them. In the latter case, the damage can keep growing until it turns into a serious injury that could force you to stop playing for a period of time. This is why a fundamental aspect of the transformation of your relationship with music needs to include becoming aware of the importance of developing an awareness of your body before, during, and after being in contact with your musical instrument. In other words, being aware of your physical metacognitive capacities in relation to playing your instrument will enhance your performance.

In my own experience as a teacher, when I ask a student what they play their instrument with, I have found the most common answers to be something like "with my arms" or, in the specific case of the violin, "holding the violin on my shoulder and neck." What a lot of responsibility for the arms, shoulders, and neck! But what about the rest of the body? For example, what role does your lower body, from the waist down, have in how you play your instrument?

The idea that we play only from the waist up places too much responsibility on the upper part of the body, resulting in a very common condition among musicians: physical tension. This is partly derived from the lack of attention we give to the overall condition of our bodies, both in and outside practice, and the lack of awareness of the lower part of the body. It is precisely this part of the body that we need to be more conscious of, because if we observe carefully, we will find that we naturally let our weight fall on the legs and feet. If you are physically tense from the legs down, your whole body will contract. Over time, this will lead to difficulties and obstacles in your playing.

It is important to be conscious of the fact that you play your instrument with your whole body, i.e., from your head right down to your toes. According to traditional Eastern medicine, every part of your body is interrelated, so tension in one area of your body will be reflected in your overall physical condition, resulting in physical ailments that can greatly affect your playing. For example, if you have a back problem, this may mean that your energy is stuck somewhere, perhaps in your hips or legs. On the other hand, if the lower part of your body is relaxed and in shape, your upper body may stop placing unnecessary pressure on it.

For a tree to grow properly, it needs deep roots, reaching far into the earth. I often offer this analogy to my students. I suggest to them that they should imagine themselves as a tree. Their body is the trunk, their feet are the roots, and their arms are the branches that the wind moves with its song. It is essential to be fully aware of your body and to learn how to listen to it. The second part of this book includes activities to help you develop body awareness in relation to playing an instrument. But for now, try the following exercise:

1. In your notebook, write down a description of your physical posture when you play your musical instrument.
2. Play a section of a piece you are studying and write down how your body reacted to your playing.
3. Describe how you would like your posture to be when you play.
4. Play the same section you chose for point two. Note whether there was any physical change when you played your instrument.

The above exercise is intended to help you observe the state of your body when you play and to recognize that good physical condition is an essential part of playing music.

Musician as Actor

A very useful strategy for the development of body awareness is to observe actors and note how they prepare physically before a rehearsal or performance. You can learn a lot from actors and how they manage their bodies. As musicians, we speak and sing through sounds. We are thus actors in sound, hence the importance of establishing more authentic contact with your body and viewing it as a part of your artistic creation.

While studying in Switzerland, I had the opportunity to participate directly in the world of theatre. Together with an actress, I performed in a play in which I portrayed an angel. Through my advice and my violin (as I acted and played at the same time), my character helped the other character find the inner strength she needed to make a crucial decision in her life. Performing in this play was an experience that changed my vision of the role of the musician and of music.

I remember that when the director told me that my character had to be barefoot throughout the whole play, I protested: how can a musician go around barefoot on the stage?! At that moment I became aware of all the prejudices I harboured, and I realized that if I really wanted to get the most out of this theatrical experience, I had to let go of my preconceived ideas. I would just let go of one to find another one arise, like the panic of seeing my violin under a spotlight, or my resistance to walking around onstage while playing. In one of the performances, while in a dialogue with the other character, my eyes froze when I saw that my violin was lying dangerously close to a small puddle of water on the stage. Fortunately, my fears were unfounded; my violin was fine. Little by little, I began to let go of my prejudices and to fully live my experience in the theatre.

As a musician, it was completely new to me. The exercises we did involved moving all over the stage with specific physical movements. This helped me experience the stage in all its magnitude for the first time, as being a classical musician, I was used to staying still in one place while performing. I became aware of the importance of sensing the whole space where an artistic creation is taking place. We also engaged in a physical warm-up before each rehearsal and each presentation. It was then that my awareness of my body began to increase and to become part of my daily violin practice. I recognized the importance of preparing physically before each practice, and the positive effects this had on my playing. I began to realize that it was not only important to improve my physical condition when playing or to learn how to move around the stage, but also, as an artist and a musician, to develop conscious body language. The quality of your playing will depend in part on the relationship you have with your body and your willingness to integrate the physical dimension into your musical performance.

The second part of this book includes physical activities to help develop a more organic and powerful relationship with the stage. But for now, try the following exercises:

1. Walk around in your socks or bare feet in a large empty space, or better still on a stage.
2. Perform a simple choreography in that space.
3. Lie down in the middle of the space. Take some deep abdominal breaths while placing your attention on the space around you.
4. Pick up your instrument and move around the space while playing it.

With this simple activity, you will begin to develop an actor's understanding of the stage, which will have a positive impact on how you play in front of an audience. You are on your way to becoming an actor in sound.

Musician as Athlete

> Menuhin became a serious yoga student, making it a regular feature of his life. Because it was not practical for Menuhin to return constantly to India to have lessons, he took Iyengar with him to Britain, France, and Switzerland. Iyengar met and taught some of the most famous artists and musicians in the world including cellist Jacqueline du Pre. They, like Menuhin, discovered that yoga releases everything... (Classic FM, 2016)

Some years ago, somebody told me that Yehudi Menuhin (1916-1999), one of the greatest violinists of the twentieth century, had described how a musician should prepare to play. He said that a musician needed the mind of a Buddhist monk and the physical condition of an athlete. This idea has become engraved in my mind, and I remember it every time I pick up my violin. It has turned into my personal catchphrase for artistic creation, as I know that the more focused my mind is, and the stronger and more relaxed my body is, the more I will enjoy the music as it emanates from within me and my musical instrument. It is as if my whole being, through the mind-body process, becomes unified with the sound. Achieving this sensation of oneness goes beyond normal experience; it is something beyond description. It simply has to be experienced personally to fully understand it.

For the past three years, I have had the pleasure of working with a teacher of Iyengar Yoga. In the past, I have tried various types of yoga, but with Iyengar Yoga I have found a clear explanation of each posture and I have been able to perform them without excessive difficulty. It has offered me the chance to rediscover the true power of my body. It is also a type of yoga in which the mind-body connection is extremely powerful.

The idea that a musician should have the physical condition of an athlete in order to play well may seem absurd at first, as musicians generally sit or stand still in one spot and do not have to exert themselves as obviously as athletes do. However, it is precisely remaining still that makes the comparison a valid one, even though the musician's muscular exertion is not as obvious as an athlete's. The misconception that musicians do not exert themselves is what leads to all kinds of tensions in the body in the short and long term. Get to know your body, look after it and love it, as it is the channel through which your most previous ideas and most profound feelings will take shape. Think of Michelangelo, who expressed his genius by using the perfect materials for the divine creation of his sculptures. Your body can be like those materials: soft enough to mold your ideas and strong enough to give them life in time and space.

> The practice of Yoga induces a primary sense of measure and proportion. Reduced to our own body, our first instrument, we learn to play it, drawing from its maximum resonance and harmony. (Menuhin, quoted in Iyengar, 2015)

Making Contact with the Wisdom of Your Body

The process of awakening an interest in musical body awareness should lead you to reflect on the following questions: Why do I feel so tense, both physically and mentally, during my daily practice? Why can playing a musical instrument cause so much stiffness?

There are various possible causes of such tension and stiffness. One is that you may be playing constantly without taking a break to rest your body. This causes your muscles to become increasingly stiff during your daily practice. Another may be constant, senseless repetition, which will be discussed in detail later in the book. The all-too-common practice of repeating a piece of music over and over can cause not only physical but also emotional and mental tension over time. As a student I often repeated a piece without knowing why I was doing it. Once I fell into this automatic habit of studying, I felt my mind become blocked, my frustration increase, and my muscles tense. It wasn't until I discovered that every problem is resolved first at the mental level that such mindless repetition was wiped off my study schedule. Sometimes it reappears, but I detect it quickly before it causes the harm it intends to cause.

The most important aim of body awareness is to create a relationship between you and your body, as you need to be conscious of your body not just during your practice, but all the time. Your physical condition plays an essential role in your instrumental technique, as your technical effectiveness will depend to a large extent on your condition.

One example of this role can be seen in the use of *vibrato*. There are many different types of *vibrato* and many ways to study it: slow, fast, from slow to fast, vice versa, etc. Of course, you need mental concentration to be able to achieve a good *vibrato*. However, good *vibrato* depends not only on studying in a certain way, but also on the relaxation of your body, which will be reflected in the tips of your fingers. When you feel tense, you face a physical blockage that will make it harder to achieve the desired technical result. On the other hand, if you focus on relaxing your body in relation to your instrument, you will be laying the technical foundations that will allow you to do things that you once thought impossible to do, including the performance of an extensive, expressive *vibrato*. It is important to see your body and its wellbeing as the basis for solid technique, a technique that will allow you to fully express what you want to express through music. At the same time, taking care of your body will contribute to your physical energy and your health.

The degree of tension or relaxation in your body has a direct effect on your nervous system. As Dr. Joe Dispenza (2007) explains, "the autonomic nervous system has two divisions, the sympathetic nervous system and the parasympathetic nervous system. Because the sympathetic nervous system prepares the body for emergencies, this part of the autonomic nervous system is sometimes called the *fight-or-flight nervous system*. When we perceive a threat from the environment, this nervous system automatically activates to get the body ready to either fight or run away. Our heart rate accelerates, blood pressure increases, respiratory rates quickens, and adrenaline is released for immediate action. At the same time, the body's energy is moved away from the digestive tract and toward the arms and legs. The sympathetic nervous system changes the body electrochemically to improve their chances for survival. Just the opposite functions are the domain of the *parasympathetic nervous system*. This division of the autonomic nervous system conserves and restores the body's energy and resources" (Dispenza, 2007, p.98). This points to the importance of body awareness in daily music practice and of achieving a physical balance when playing your musical instrument. This will allow you to shift from survival mode to a state of total harmony, a state in which your true capacities as a musician will amaze you.

There are various techniques that can help foster an awareness of your body and to achieve greater physical relaxation when playing. These include yoga, tai chi, pilates, chi kung, and the Alexander Technique. The Alexander Technique is especially good for musicians seeking to develop their physical fitness and correct their posture, as it is based on re-harmonizing your whole body through specific exercises. This re-harmonization also has a very positive and healthy impact on your mind. While I was studying in Switzerland, I had the opportunity to take classes in the Alexander Technique. In fact, thanks to these classes, I was able to recover from the physical injury I'd been suffering from at that time. Curiously, after taking the course, another student at the conservatory commented that I looked taller! It was as if through this technique I had recovered my true physical condition, characterized by fitness, wellbeing, and a state of relaxed alertness. The Alexander Technique is an effective way of establishing an awareness of your body's balance, posture, and coordination, and of the relationship between body and mind.

Richard Brennan (1992) describes the effects of the incorrect use of the body, as well as the benefits of using it consciously. "When you use your body incorrectly, your tension increases, your thoughts are rigid and harmful, and you feel frustration and disappointment. Conversely, when you are aware of your body, your tension decreases, there is harmony and balance in every part of your life, your mind is more open, and you feel happiness and wellbeing" (Brennan, 1992, p.109). It is these effects of full body awareness that will lay a solid foundation for a musical technique free of any kind of tension.

Another essential element for the physical development of music students is the instruction in physical expression offered at some music schools around the world. It is just as important to prepare the body for playing as the development of your physical connection with your instrument. In a way, musicians could be considered performers who dance to their musical performances in a conscious way. Vika Kleiman (2012), who teaches somatic education at Escola Superior de Música de Catalunya, describes the function of bodily expression in her teaching very clearly when she explains that "the work I propose in my courses in bodily expression is an invitation to students to meet their own bodies and experience it in a unique way, allowing them to create an experience in which new forms and new bodies are possible." (Kleiman, 2012, p.6). The next chapter will explore the importance of bodily expression in playing a musical instrument in more detail.

Observing yourself not only while studying but during all your activities can be a very useful strategy for the development of body awareness. As an exercise you can start taking time to monitor your body in different situations. For example, try observing your posture while you're washing dishes, waiting in a queue, or in any other everyday activity. Take note of whether your shoulders are tense or relaxed, whether your back is straight, whether you're letting your weight fall on your feet, whether your neck is relaxed. At the same time, paying attention to the energy around your body (divergent attention) can help you relax. The concept of divergent attention is discussed in the second part of this book, as part of the process of meditation.

Being conscious of your body at all times will keep your mind alert. This will contribute to the healthy correction of your physical posture and to a greater internal balance. You will start feeling huge benefits, which will be reflected in all your activities.

The second part of this book includes specific exercises to prepare your body for practising with your instrument every day, and exercises to keep your body in good condition during and after each practice. To begin this process, you can do the exercise outlined above of taking conscious notice of your body, of the energy around it, and of your breathing at different times, as even this simple exercise can help you start to feel a difference in muscle tone when playing your instrument.

The main objective of the ideas described above is to change your perception of your body. Many musicians suffer from muscle tensions when playing an instrument, ranging from mild to severe. And in many cases those tensions become a musician's natural physical condition. This is why you need to re-educate your body through relaxation and toning exercises, so that you can get used to feeling tension-free. This feeling will totally change your perception of your body when you play. It is possible that after engaging in this kind of body awareness even the most minimal tension can affect you, tension that previously would have gone by completely unnoticed. This is something that I personally began to experience after I began taking consciousness of my physical condition at all times. It was as if as soon as any tension arose my body would whisper in my ear: "Hey, I don't recognize this. Take me back to my normal condition!"

To understand this more clearly, try the following exercise:

1. Sit down in a chair with your knees positioned slightly lower than your waist. Try to keep your back as straight and relaxed as possible. Feel how all your weight falls on your feet, which should be planted firmly on the floor.
2. Start taking note of where you have tension and try to relax that specific part of your body by breathing deeply.
3. Place your attention on the energy around each part of your body. You can start at the feet and work your way through your body until you get to the top of your head, trying to release the tension everywhere you find it. At the end of the exercise, breathe in deeply, and on exhaling, let out the sound "aaah", imagining that all the tension is leaving your body. Ending the exercise this way will bring a sense of total relief.
4. Choose a piece of music and play it.
5. Write down your reflections.

This exercise is excellent for identifying the amount of tension stored in your body and also for recognizing the power that you have to relax your body and release the tensions accumulated in it.

In this way, you can become an observer of your own body, which will help you play your instrument with more freedom and expression. When you listen to your body and its inner sensations you will automatically be bringing it into harmony.

By now you may be thinking: "but it sounds like a lot of work!" That is a normal reaction, as this is a study method that may initially require a physical, emotional, and mental transformation of your relationship with your instrument and with music. However, if this book has fallen into your hands and awakened a need in you to change something in your perspective on the world of music, be patient and persevere. Try to change at your own pace and according to your own needs, but always with dedication and enthusiasm. You will see wonderful results that in one way or another will influence your musical world creatively and positively.

1.7. THE SONIC IMPULSE

A body condition that is open to precepts (new ways of seeing and hearing), affects (new ways of feeling and experiencing) and concepts (new ways of thinking and knowing). (Kesselman, 2003, quoted by Kleiman, 2019)

"Serious" Music

The physical stiffness suffered by so many musicians in the world of classical music raises a number of interesting questions. Consider one of the most common events associated with classical music: a recital. Normally, the audience is seated practically the whole time in a comfortable (or not so comfortable) seat, and their bodies move very little or not at all throughout the event. The musician comes out onto the stage, takes up a fixed position, and remains in that position throughout the whole performance. What can we conclude from this? Obviously, there is a severe lack of musical-body movement, suggesting that the musician and audience are not feeling the music in their physical beings and allowing that feeling to manifest itself. This perhaps has its origins in the general idea that classical music is "serious music". But what does this mean exactly? Does it mean that we must experience it coldly and without any commitment to establishing a true relationship with the music? Or that because it has a long history behind it, we must treat it with complete and utter solemnity? Of course, it is important for musicians and music listeners to cultivate a knowledge of musical history and include it in their learning in order to enrich their experience of the world of music. However, this doesn't mean that we have to experience classical music in a purely detached, analytical way.

If you compare classical music with other forms of sonic expression, you will find a huge difference in this respect. Take for example a blues concert. Here, both performers and audience move to the rhythm of the melodies of these profound and moving songs. For some reason, this is something permitted in this music genre.

Similarly, in pop music, perhaps the extreme opposite of the classical genre, the singers move all over the stage and engage the members of their audience, who are dancing constantly to their songs.

I don't mean to suggest with these comparisons that a classical music recital can or should be turned into a rock concert. My intention is simply to open up a topic that will prompt reflection on the different ways of achieving a greater, more natural engagement with the world of music. Perhaps it is time to become more conscious of this point and to find new ways of expressing our art, new ways of responding to the power of the music with our whole being. Let's allow the sound to inspire us to make our own "choreographies" both as performers and as listeners. Let's allow our bodies to relax and breathe by being in contact with classical music. In this way, we will be able to perceive its true power within us and—most importantly of all—to begin enjoying it in all its splendour. Such an approach could have the effect of transforming a classical music concert in a way that intensifies the performer-audience-space relationship through the connection between sound and movement. These and other possibilities are worth reflecting on.

> It is not about abandoning the teaching of technique; of course, technique is essential, but always as a means to achieve expressive ends. (Pozo, 2020)

Music and Movement

There are various disciplines of movement that involve creating choreographies based on music, such as ballet, contemporary dance, and tango. Another is eurythmy, created in the early twentieth century out of a collaboration between dancers and the Austrian philosopher Rudolf Steiner, which has a very close connection with the music as its movements represent the elements of classical music in a very precise way. For example, a movement may represent a specific note, a key change, or a chord. In its own way, eurythmy very faithfully expresses the forms of the music in space. But in addition, it is also a branch of modern dance that emerged in the time of Isadora Duncan (1877-1927), and it shares her innovative approach of creating movements based on emotional responses. In other words, the action is the result of a specific feeling. This is clear in the performance of an "A" in eurythmy; it is not merely a mechanical movement in which you open your arms in a certain way as it symbolizes an opening of ourselves to the world.

I have personally had the opportunity of having a direct experience with eurythmy, as while studying in Lugano I was able to participate in various courses. I recall that the movement that represented the "A" was extremely difficult for me, but over time this kind of dance began to have a very positive effect on my inner world. I found I could truly experience the emotional changes that occur when moving between different elements of music, such as a shift from a major to a minor key. In eurythmy, a major key represents an openness to the outside world, while a minor key elicits a reflection on our inner worlds. Apart from the courses, I also had the opportunity to perform Franck's Sonata in A Minor for violin and piano together with a eurythmist. It was a fantastic experience. Playing music for this kind of dance can help you feel the underlying theme of a piece of music, as if some mysterious force draws you into the sound.

Participating in a discipline of movement can open up a sensory perception that can be extremely beneficial to your playing. And it can be even more beneficial for musicians to interact with these disciplines, not only as spectators or accompanists but as an integral part of a dance performance. This can be a highly effective strategy both for releasing tensions when playing and for enjoying a whole new experience of the stage.

I enjoyed such an experience myself when I worked with a contemporary dancer in a multidisciplinary event. In this event I came out onto the stage playing my violin as a character who, coincidentally, was a violinist. For the performance I was required to move around the whole stage and to interact with the dancer. There is a huge difference between playing while standing or sitting still in one place and playing as a character who is "dancing" around the space. Everything changes. The musical intentions, the sound itself, the rhythms—everything. There is no time to think about your apparent limitations, as you become a part of the story and it will only work when you're thinking as the character that you are playing at that moment. This sensation forces your mind to focus on the present, on the action of the moment. Your brainwaves shift from beta (alert state) to alpha (creative state).

What I learned from this experience is how our bodies naturally respond to the sound of the music with physical impulses, and how this can contribute to experiencing the world of music in a freer and more enjoyable way. This doesn't necessarily mean you have to take up dancing or to make exaggerated movements with your body when playing. It is simply about opening a window of possibility to the incorporation of conscious movement into your musical performance in order to enhance the fluidity of your playing. Awakening this consciousness of movement will help you to move together with the music you are playing rather than against it. If every action in your performance emerges from a need for expression, our physical impulses will be in total harmony with your musical instrument, with the sound, the rhythms, and the dynamics of the works you are playing. In a way, we all "dance" when we play an instrument. What we need to do is to turn this dancing into another strategy for our artistic development.

To better understand the above, try the following exercise:

1. Choose a piece of music that you like.
2. Before listening to it, take some slow, deep breaths and ensure that nothing and nobody will interrupt you.
3. Listen to the piece with the intention of NOT analyzing it. Allow your whole being to listen to it; your mind, heart, and body.

4. When you're finished, listen to the piece again. This time, allow the upper part of your body to react with natural movements to each part of the piece.

5. Finally, listen to the piece one more time, this time allowing your whole body to respond naturally to the music. Let your natural impulses be awakened by the sound.

When doing this exercise, try to move in response to what the music suggests to you rather than simply moving for its own sake. The idea is to allow your body to truly experience the content of the music you're listening to. It is also a good idea to keep breathing slowly and deeply throughout the exercise, as the mind-emotions-body relationship is central to this exercise and your breathing is what makes this relationship possible. The importance of breathing will be discussed in detail in the next chapter.

The objective of these kinds of exercises is to foster a need to experience the music in your whole being, to make it a part of your essence and to reduce any space that may exist between you and the music so that it can take root in your inner world. This is a learning process that develops a musician's creative competence and capacity to embody sound itself.

Another exercise that can contribute to the sound-impulse relationship is as follows:

1. Choose a melody from the work you are studying.
2. Find a place where you won't be interrupted and take some slow, deep abdominal breaths.
3. Bring the melody you chose to mind.
4. Let your body react naturally while playing the melody in your mind. Think of it as a small and simple choreography.

You can carry out this sequence with the different melodies of your piece. You will start to feel that the sound has the ability to mold both our emotions and our physical movements. This exercise is an excellent strategy not only for enhancing your musical sensibility but also for informing your body that it can be relaxed, toned, and in harmony with the world of sound. Over time, this will be reflected positively in your playing. You will be more aware of the fact that technique is not separate from the music, but a physical means through which you can express your musical ideas in a captivating way.

At first you may feel uncomfortable doing this kind of exercise; this is totally normal. Just remember that nobody is watching you or judging you. You are alone with yourself and the music, which will be guiding you toward relaxing your inner world, which will in time have a very positive impact on your outer world and thus on all your actions.

Playing an instrument challenges us constantly to confront ourselves. It is a faithful reflection of what is happening in our lives and a marvelous teacher for those who like transformations. Remember that music is something that emanates from within us. It is where your true strength as a performer is found.

Bodily Expression at Schools of Music

Training in bodily expression is becoming an increasingly prominent component of music programs around the world. The importance of movement for playing a musical instrument cannot be ignored, as it is a key element in the transformation of the music school system. Establishing a relationship between music and movement is essential for musicians to find a way of expressing their musical ideas freely and effectively.

The Escola di Música di Catalunya (ESMUC) is one of the institutions introducing body movement into their curricula with a course teaching the physical dimension of music. Vika Kleiman (2019) clearly defines the objectives of this course: to discover the musicality of your body with sound and in silence, in relation to music and without it. To recognize your own movement and your own sound. To be able to compose small stage arrangements that link music and dance. To experiment with the possibility of creating music and movement improvisations alone and in a group (Kleiman, 2019).

These objectives reflect the importance of recognizing our bodies as instruments, acknowledging our physical creativity in relation to both sound and silence. Movement is associated with an emotional state that will be conveyed through an action involving the body and sound, which can be achieved through improvisation.

Improvising with your body and with music is much more complex than might be imagined. As Kleiman (2019) points out, "free improvisation is not, as I have sometimes heard, 'just doing anything'. It requires precise training and commitment to be able to explore 'ways of doing' through the instrument, as well as understanding that instrument in depth—whether it be your body or your musical instrument—so that you can expand the possibilities and strategies both of sound and of movement (Kleiman, 2019).

This idea points to a new way of teaching a musical instrument and the need for us as teachers to transform our pedagogical approach through the integration of a physical perspective. For many years, "technique" has been understood as hours and hours of study and scales. Of course, these two aspects of learning an instrument are important for a student's development. But to study pieces and practice scales over and over can often cause students tension and even injuries.

With the above in mind, we need to understand physical fitness and creativity as the foundation for a sound and effective technique that will enable students to express themselves clearly. This will give them a technique consisting of precise and conscious physical movements and a truly expressive performance. But in addition, we also need to understand musical elements like phrasing and dynamics from the perspective of the combination of music and movement. Students can experience this through the development of creative awareness by using physical and musical improvisation and assigning movements to different classical pieces.

During a teaching residence at the Music in the Alps Festival in Bad Gastein, Austria in 2018, I had the opportunity to try combining music and movement in my classes.

While working with one of the students on a piece of music she was practising, we developed specific physical movements to accompany the piece. In other words, she performed a simple choreography while playing the piece. In this way, she gained a sensory understanding of the meaning of a clear, expressive phrasing. It was a kind of epiphany for her, as she perceived the phrasing of the piece on a physical level. The result was a performance with a profound and clear musicality. This had a decisive influence on how she played the piece, and on her posture while playing. Prior to this, we had engaged in improvisations with music and movement that had completely changed her relationship with her body and her body's relationship with her musical instrument. Her body language while playing became stronger and freer, resulting in a captivating performance.

The second part of this book outlines some activities involving music and movement. But for now, try the following exercise to help apply your metacognitive capacities of musical creation to your daily practice:

1. Choose a section of a piece you are studying.
2. Improvise a choreography while listening to that section in your mind.
3. With your musical instrument, perform an improvisation combining music and movement.
4. Now play the section of the piece while moving around the space.
5. Write down your reflections.

The above exercise will help give your playing a quality of profound, genuine freedom. We are athletes, actors, and dancers of sound in action.

Mirrors

Not long ago I had the opportunity to perform in a dance and music show titled *Mirrors*. The musical accompaniment was J. S. Bach's Sonata in G Minor and some avant-garde pieces I had composed. It was the first time that I had played classical music and avant-garde music together in an interdisciplinary context of this kind. At the same time, the dancer and I had the wonderful experience of being guided by a theatre director.

The performance of Bach's sonata was an especially big challenge. It was the first time in my career that I had to play a piece of Baroque music while portraying a character. The dancer's choreography had a big influence on the way I played. It was as if her movements were molding each phrase of the sonata. I myself also performed a simple choreography while playing Bach. These movements (both the dancer's and my own) guided my performance and created specific emotions to convey.

Working with a theatre director meant I had to think about the reason behind each phrase and its significance for the story in *Mirrors*. It was a fascinating process. My whole being was engaged with the story while I played, and my mind, emotions, and body became a single unit through which the message of *Mirrors* was transmitted to the audience. I became a sonic character on stage.

Without doubt, working with a dancer throughout the process of developing and presenting *Mirrors* constituted a new chapter in my career as an artist and as a teacher. Teaching and experiencing music through movement is an essential part of the transformation of music education. The second part of this book includes activities designed to develop an awareness of music and movement in your work as an artist.

> I don't know whether the development of the teacher's sensory intelligence requires a special kind of work, physical exercise, but it certainly requires a "transvaluation", a search. Teachers who are used to conveying concepts far removed from the experiences that produced them, from the experiences that gave them life, will have to reinvent them in their bodies. The vibratile body will be the instrument of a new neutrality. (Kesselman, 2003)

1.8. BREATHING: THE SOURCE OF THE BODY'S SOUND

> When the breath wanders, the mind also is unsteady. But when the breath is calmed, the mind too will be still, and the yogi achieves long life. Therefore, one should learn to control the breath. (Svatmarama, quoted in Brulé, 2018 p.73)

Breathing Right

Conscious breathing as part of playing an instrument is a topic seldom touched upon in music teaching. In general, when we think about breathing, we think about doing it with our lungs. We might take a breath before playing, but after a while breathing becomes a forgotten topic.

This is very common in the world of music teaching, as the need to breathe while playing music rarely forms part of any music program. This is why I have chosen to include a chapter especially dedicated to this important issue. By breathing right, you can help transform your physical perception from one of tension to one of complete relaxation. This will have a very positive influence both on the quality of your mental focus and on your artistic performance.

Breathing in Daily Practice

All life around us is propelled by breath. It is breath that keeps all of nature's creatures alive. Without breath, there would be no life. We experience breath right from the beginning, even in the mother's womb. When we are babies, we breathe naturally with our abdomens. But as time passes, we begin to lose this ability that nature has given us, and then tensions begin to appear. Only when we sleep does our body remember this normal way of breathing.

Breathing calms us and relaxes our joints and muscles. This is why we often tell people to breathe deeply when they are upset or when they are going to give a speech. But when people tell us to breathe deeply, our tendency is to breathe with the chest, not with the abdomen. The difference between the two is that breathing from the lungs can be limited and less effective in fostering body awareness than abdominal breathing. Breathing from the abdomen is deeper and easier to control, making its effect truly relaxing and toning.

Breathing properly not only tones the body but also improves your sensitivity to sound. If you watch professional singers carefully, you will notice that they breathe continually with their abdomens when singing. For these performers, breathing is an extremely important technical strategy.

Incorporating breathing into your daily practice will help you experience the world of sound more intensely and vibrantly, as sound finds its physical resonance in our abdominal breathing. In other words, your "sound" emerges from your abdominal region. This way of perceiving the importance of conscious breathing will bring your whole being into harmony with the world of sound. Through your breathing, your essence will be united with the essence of the music. When you breathe, the music breathes too. That's why it is so important to find this point of physical contact between yourself and the world of sound.

Breathing directly affects both the sympathetic and parasympathetic nervous systems. When we lose control over our breathing, the effects on the sympathetic nervous system, like stress, become obvious. On the other hand, when we breathe consciously, the effects on the parasympathetic nervous system, like relaxation, are felt in the body.

As Dan Brulé points out, when you control your breath, you can intentionally influence your brain and autonomic nervous system and literally change your mind-body state. By changing the pattern of your breath, you change the pattern of the information that is sent to the brain (Brulé, 2018, p.30). This highlights the importance of breathing on the physical and neural level.

The following is a breathing technique in yoga that can help achieve balance between the sympathetic and parasympathetic nervous system:

While seated in a chair with your back straight and your feet on the floor, place your thumb over your right nostril. Breathe in slowly for four beats through your left nostril, then cover your left nostril with your little finger and breathe out for four beats through the right nostril. Repeat this sequence eight times. Write down your observations.

This is an excellent exercise to use five minutes before a public performance.

Meditation is an excellent strategy for achieving physical and mental equilibrium through slow, deep, abdominal breathing, as it helps the brain shift from beta to alpha. Beta brainwaves bring about an alert state while alpha brainwaves elicit a state of creative physical and mental relaxation. If you are already familiar with a breathing technique, great! If not, you can start practising it simply and effectively in the following way:

1. Sit in a chair for a few minutes every day, either at dawn or in the evening, with your back straight and your feet planted firmly on the floor, and with the palms of your hands over your thighs. You can also meditate while kneeling, provided your back is straight. Find the posture that works best for you.
2. Once you have found the right posture, focus your attention on your slow, deep abdominal breathing through your nose.

3. Place your attention on each part of your body, beginning with your head and ending with your feet. As you scan your body, direct your mind to the energy around each part of your body.
4. Don't analyze or hold onto the thoughts that come to your mind. Simply let them go and place your attention on the flow of your breathing.
5. When you're done, cross your hands over the centre of your chest and breathe slowly for six beats, hold it for four beats, and then breathe out for six more.

Practising these activities every day will help you begin to perceive that your breathing is the crucial link between your mind and your body. Your body will relax, and your mental focus will increase. This is also time that you will be able to dedicate to being with yourself, as a way of recharging your batteries for another day.

When done properly, abdominal breathing is a key element for enhancing your physical sensations when you play your instrument. Moreover, regardless of your level of physical tension, breathing in this way will help you experience your body differently, freeing you of tension and stiffness. And not only will you be consciously raising your body to a state of wellbeing, but you will also find that your focus when playing will be much better.

Ironically, when we know that a difficult passage in the piece we are playing is coming up, our tension increases and we stop breathing regularly, when in fact it should be the other way around, as this is precisely the type of situation where we need to be breathing deeply.

To experience what has been described above, try out the following exercise:

1. Find a peaceful and quiet place.
2. Choose a passage of music that requires some dramatic changes of position. Play the passage three times without stopping.
3. Observe your muscle tone and listen to your sound and tuning. Write down your reflections.
4. Place a yoga mat or blanket on the floor and lie down on it. Keep your body straight, with the palms of your hands upward, and feel how you relax on the floor with each breath.
5. While breathing this way, imagine that your stomach is like a balloon that inflates upon inhaling and deflates upon exhaling. Put your hand on your abdomen so you can feel the gentle movements caused by your deep breathing. Inhale for four slow beats and exhale for four slow beats. Pause for two beats between each inhalation and exhalation, holding your breath on each pause. Do the first inhalations and exhalations

through your nose, then inhale through your nose and exhale through your mouth, letting out an "aaaaahhh" sound.

6. Repeat this breathing several times, relaxing your body and mind (without falling asleep!).
7. Now raise yourself up on one side slowly and pick up your instrument. Play the same passage again, maintaining the same abdominal breathing. Before each repetition, breathe with your abdomen and imagine every detail of yourself playing the passage easily.
8. When finished, make some notes on your experience.

This exercise is excellent for reminding us that we actually play our instruments with our whole bodies, and that a relaxed and flexible body is the basis for a solid and effective technique. This is why what you felt in the second part of the exercise was no doubt quite different from what you felt in the first. For the second part, you relaxed your body, while at the same time toning it up, and so your playing became more fluid and natural. You may have noticed a small or a large difference between the first and second parts of the exercise. But if you use these exercises on a regular basis, you will notice substantial changes in your way of playing in terms of your physical relationship with your instrument and your mental focus.

Here's another effective exercise to incorporate conscious breathing into your playing:

1. Adopt the posture you normally hold when playing your instrument, but without your instrument.
2. While in this position, concentrate your attention on deep and relaxed breathing. Observe how your breathing relaxes your body.
3. Now, do the same thing again, but this time with your instrument in your hands. If you keep breathing the same way, you'll feel the sensation of relaxation you achieved in step two.
4. Make some simple, long sounds. Keep your concentration on your breathing.
5. Write down your observations.

The effect of this exercise is very powerful. With your breathing, you're telling your mind that your posture while playing can be relaxed. In other words, you are sending new signals to your brain about how you play your instrument. This in turn can have very positive results in terms of your physical condition while playing, as you are guiding your body towards a new body-instrument relationship, one that is free of tensions. You are conditioning your body to embrace a new way of playing.

At the physical level, learning to breathe properly will begin to broaden and relax the muscles of your back. According to the traditional Asian therapy known as *shiatsu*, tensions in the shoulders can be a sign of a blockage in the stomach. This is why breathing from the abdomen can be important for freeing up the movement of your arms, shoulders, and neck, as you will be unblocking the cause of the tension. In addition, all your weight will fall naturally on your feet, which will relax the upper part of your body. Abdominal breathing is a source of energy distribution that can fill your whole body with vitality. This is a very important concept in *shiatsu*, which has a specific name for the abdominal region: the *hara*. The *hara* symbolizes a point of power in our body which, when flowing properly, centres us on our actions so that they can positively reflect our true mental and emotional capacities.

Breathing Techniques

If you want to learn more about proper, effective breathing, it is advisable to take lessons with experts on the subject, such as masters in disciplines like yoga, tai chi, qigong, hara breathing, breath work, or Wim Hof breathing.

There are also specific courses for learning how to breathe properly—what is known as hara breathing. Such courses can be extraordinarily effective as they focus on abdominal breathing in such a way that you will learn how to apply this type of breathing naturally, not only before playing but also while playing your instrument.

As mentioned above, if you want to explore an abdominal breathing technique more deeply it is advisable to do so under the instruction of a professional in the field. Nevertheless, right from this moment you can start being more aware of your breathing not only while studying but also in your everyday activities, as this will increase your ability to breathe naturally through your abdomen. In this way, abdominal breathing will become a natural part of your playing. Think of breathing as a magic touch in your music practice that has the power to unify your mind, emotions, and body with the world of sound, so that you and the music can become one.

Knowing how to breathe is so powerful that it can even help you establish a purer and more authentic level of contact with your audience, as your breathing will make the music flow even better in space, reaching the heart of the listener and creating an energy that is truly captivating.

1.9. SOUND

Sound is an entity that travels in space, beyond time... its essence resonates inside me, evoking its eternal presence and my own... (Anonymous)

What Is Sound?

Perhaps you've been playing an instrument for years, attending concerts for years, teaching classes, or playing in an ensemble and interacting with other musicians for years. You've been creating sounds constantly, to the point that it has turned into something totally "ordinary and normal" to be in contact with the world of sound every day.

But imagine that after giving a concert, you are approached by a six-year-old who was captivated by your performance, who asks you: "What comes out of your instrument?"

"Well," you reply, "what comes out is a musical sound."

"Sound?" asks the child with a look of wonder. "But what is that? What is sound?"

"Well," you explain, "sound is a series of vibrations... waves that travel in space, produced by the musical instrument..."

And you continue to offer a technical definition of sound as best as you can. But the child merely looks at you in dismay as if to say: "Yes, but what is sound really? Where does it come from? Why did I like the sound that came out of your instrument so much?"

An encounter like this might be easily forgotten after a while. Or perhaps the image of that child's look of curiosity about sound will stay in your mind, along with her question: What is sound?

If the child's innocent question prompts you to reflect on the essence of sound, it means you're ready to think about sound in a different way, a way that will enrich your relationship with that amazing and profound world that we call music.

A New Approach to the Essence of Sound

From the perspective of physics, sound is a set of waves and vibrations produced by a medium at a particular frequency. The frequency that the human ear can apparently perceive ranges from twenty to twenty thousand hertz. This explanation, while totally valid in itself, offers a point of departure for going beyond it.

First of all, consider the phrase: "sound is a set of waves and vibrations produced by a medium." What exactly do we mean by "a medium"? And what do these "waves and vibrations" consist of? In our particular case, a musical instrument offers a clear example of a medium that produces vibrations and waves that travel in space. This is also a valid explanation, but what we now need to do is go beyond this physical concept. With this in mind, try the following exercise:

1. Find a quiet place where you won't be interrupted.
2. Have your musical instrument on hand.
3. Sit in a chair with your back as straight as possible and your feet planted firmly on the floor.
4. Take some slow abdominal breaths (this will help you relax your mind and body). Keep breathing this way throughout the exercise.
5. Close your eyes and imagine an element of nature (e.g., the movement of the branches of a tree in the wind). Try to imagine it in as much detail as possible.
6. Take note of the physical, mental, and emotional sensations that this image provokes in you.
7. Take your instrument and play a series of sounds that express the image you chose. Try to hold on to the sensations provoked by the image while you play.
8. When you're done, hold your playing position in silence for a moment and slowly lower your hands.
9. When you feel ready, write down how you felt during the exercise and how you experienced the sound you made.

If during this exercise you found it hard to conjure up a detailed image as suggested, don't worry; this comes with practice. For the moment what is important is to start hearing sound in relation to an element of nature on the mental level.

The objectives of this exercise, which you should try doing for a few minutes in each practice, are:

➢ To be able to hear the sound of an element of nature in your mind.
➢ To be conscious of your abdominal breathing.
➢ To learn to experience sound around you and inside you.
➢ To try to capture in your playing the mental, physical, and emotional sensation provoked by the image.

If carried out every day, the power of this simple exercise can help you perceive sound in a different way and to play music more naturally. This exercise can also help you experience for yourself how sound originates from a place outside your musical instrument. The chapters that follow detail other exercises of this kind.

For me, the image of the wind is an excellent starting point for this type of exercise. Imagining the sound of the wind, like the mysterious howl of a gale on a winter's night, can relax you in a way that can create a sensation of floating while you play the sounds that represent it. I have found this to be the case when trying this exercise with several students of mine. When they hold this image in their minds, a specific emotion is evoked that has the effect of correcting their posture naturally. Upon performing this exercise, their minds, emotions, and bodies become one, and when they play, they produce a truly moving sonic expression.

Having experienced sound from another perspective, let's return now to the statement that "sound is a set of waves and vibrations produced by a medium."

In the context of music, the medium referred to here is the medium of nature itself. The waves and vibrations are the voice of nature, which finds its resonance in you and your playing. In this way, nature expresses its deepest mysteries through your art.

A New Way of Perceiving the World of Sound

This is but one of many interpretations of the concept of sound. In this case, the function of such an explanation is precisely to expand your vision of the world of sound so as to enrich your artistic journey and your musical performances. Stopping for a moment to perceive sound in a different way can give your daily study greater meaning and force. In this way, you will be creating a consciousness of sound, which is essential in the process of transformation of your daily practice. If you want to achieve an authentic, captivating performance for a particular audience, free of any kind of tension, you first need to transform how you practice at home. This transformation takes place by engaging in a more profound way with sound itself.

In its purest and most elevated essence, sound is a vibrating bridge between us and the natural world. This brings to mind one of the answers given to that six-year-old child: "sound is a vibration that travels in space". Yes, this was in fact the right answer; only now, through your desire to go beyond an abstract concept, you have begun to experience that answer on a sensory level.

All of this is leading towards a new way of perceiving the world of sound. It is a perception that can make us conscious of sound as the fundamental element of human nature that brings us into contact with our deepest essence. Once we are conscious of this, we have no other option than to begin to explore the true mission of music, and our mission as interpreters of the vast and magical world of sound. We need to always be searching for the beauty of sound in every musical performance. In this way, we can crack the mystery of sound itself.

> ... True sound arises from complete calm, from pure silence... let us allow this calm to live so that it may bring to life those beautiful sounds that reside, and have always resided, in the very depths of our hearts... (Anonymous)

The Role of Improvisation in Music Education

Musical improvisation is a subject that has received very little attention in classical music education. When we think of improvisation, we tend to think of musical genres like jazz or blues rather than classical music. This is partly due to the fact that classical musicians are accustomed to reading a score to be able to create a sonic world with their instruments.

It is worth recalling, however, that in the Baroque period musicians were expected to enrich the works they performed by adding their own flourishes. This practice disappeared during the classical period. Today, there are musicians with classical training who improvise with genres like avant-garde music. However, in post-secondary classical music schools, improvisation is not a subject that receives much attention.

In a seminar I gave some years ago, I asked one participant to create a rhythm on a drum. She found it hard to do because she felt shy and afraid that she might "not do it right." I guided her by suggesting she hold an image of nature in her mind. Her next attempt was much freer and more creative. This experience made me think about our expectations in classical music education that everything needs to be perfect, an idea that leaves no room for our own creativity. Improvisation can play an important role in the development of students' creative skills, which in turn can enhance their performances of classical pieces.

In my own experience as a violinist and artist, I have often made use of improvisation as a means of free and natural expression. I first discovered this possibility while studying in Switzerland. When I improvised, I felt more in touch with the violin and with the world of sound than when I played the classical pieces I was working on. By moving back and forth between improvised avant-garde music and classical music I reached a point where I felt a balance between the two genres and where each one greatly enriched the other.

On the mental level, when you improvise, your analytical mind is completely silenced and you establish a connection between your conscious and unconscious mind. The freedom of improvising automatically creates a harmonious connection between you and your musical instrument. Your mind shifts into an alpha state of creativity and your body responds in a more natural way. On the other hand, playing a classical piece triggers your analytical mind, the part of your brain that wants to control everything, and the creative process can therefore sometimes be blocked. In such cases, your brain is in beta or high beta state. Many years ago, during a class with my second violin teacher in Switzerland, I played a classical piece and then improvised. When I finished, she observed: "When you improvise, your technical skills flow so well. This is what needs to happen in classical music." When I improvised, my brain shifted into an alpha state, bringing together my conscious and subconscious minds so that my playing could flow more freely. But when playing the classical piece, my mind shifted into a high beta state, a state of stress, and my body didn't respond in the same way as it did when I improvised. However, once you discover this portal of creativity and see the results on the physical level, you will be able to transfer these sensations to your performances of classical works.

In my experience as a teacher, I have witnessed students, from beginners through to advanced, experience a very different relationship with their musical instrument when they try creating their own music. And the level of their creativity is impressive. They can even rise to much higher technical challenges than they can while practising a classical piece.

Younger students respond immediately and wonderfully to improvisation, exhibiting technical abilities far beyond their level. Before the age of twelve, their brains are still predominantly in alpha state, and thus the connection between their minds and bodies is more harmonious. They also display an extraordinary level of creativity and freedom while they explore all the possibilities of their instrument.

In light of the above, it is high time that classical music programs began to include improvisation as a subject. It is clearly a powerful strategy for the development of a student's artistic capacities.

Try the following activities to experience the power of improvisation for your own musical creativity:

1. Lie down on a yoga mat or something similar.
2. Inhale for six beats, hold your breath for six beats, exhale for six beats, and hold again for six beats. Repeat this sequence eight times.
3. When you finish, stretch your arms up over your head, stretch out your toes, and return to your starting position. Carry out this sequence five times.
4. Take your instrument in your hands and raise it to a playing position. Focus your attention on the middle of your chest. Breathe deeply.
5. Bring to mind an image that can inspire a specific emotion in you.
6. With your attention still on the middle of your chest, begin playing a series of sounds while moving around the room.
7. At the end of your creative experience, write down your reflections.

This type of activity will not only develop your metacognitive skills of creation but will also help you develop a healthy and profound relationship with the essence of the world of sound. Improvisation allows the sound to enter you naturally, in a state in which your brain waves are in alpha.

Another creative way of experiencing this is by improvising together with others. This can trigger an even greater release of spontaneous musicality. Creating sounds with other musicians will enrich your metacognitive skills of creation even more. It is a form of teamwork that is key to the development of each student's musicality. To better understand this idea, try the following group activities:

1. Find another music student with which to do this activity.
2. Lie down on yoga mats side by side.
3. Inhale for six beats, hold for four, and then exhale for another six beats.
4. Pick up your instruments and raise them to a playing position.
5. Begin your improvisation while moving around the room.
6. When you're done, write down your reflections.

These activities foster a more profound and authentic relationship between the performer and the world of sound. This relationship is fundamental to the process of learning to play classical music.

The activities will also help you change your perception of your mission as a performing artist. The next section deals with a key aspect in this process of transforming how we teach and learn a musical instrument: our system of beliefs about playing music.

1.10. A PROFOUND TRANSFORMATION

How we see ourselves will affect every moment of our musical performances. It is thus in our minds where the changes to our vision of our role as artists need to take place to create the musicians that our hearts are calling for us to be. (Anonymous)

A Change to our Vision of Music

The aim of this chapter is to help you reflect on your current relationship with the world of music, your instrument, and yourself. This reflection will lay the foundations for a transformation of your relationship with the art of sound.

The challenge in changing your view of music is making the change from the inside out and not the other way around. This is a challenge, because we normally rely on external influences to change how we view things.

At first, this new way of studying, or creating, may seem like a lot of work, as we're used to a mode of study in which we don't use our full potential as human beings. This potential is like a muscle which, as it hasn't been used fully, takes time to get working and to yield clear results. But with persistence and dedication, these results can be wonderful.

The transformation of your way of playing needs to first happen at the mental level, because your mind holds the key to a complete change of your self-image as an artist. This is a concept that may seem abstract at first. This is why it needs to be experienced directly to understand the magnitude of its effects.

To better understand this idea, try the exercise below:

1. Find a quiet place where you won't be interrupted.
2. Take some slow, deep breaths to shift your brain into a relaxed, alpha state.
3. Close your eyes and imagine yourself playing, picturing the scene in detail. Observe the movements of your body in relation to your instrument, the sensations produced by your playing, and your focus on what you're doing. It is important to ensure that you imagine this scene from your own point of view and not as if you were looking at yourself from outside. In this way you can visualize exactly how you are playing.
4. When you're done, write a description in your notebook of the scene you saw in your mind of yourself playing. Be as detailed as possible. Write about both your physical position and your emotions and mental state while playing.

This is an extremely interesting exercise because it can help us realize that the way we play our instruments, even at the physical level, is based on the idea we have of ourselves as musicians. Moreover, during the exercise, you could probably see what you like about your playing and what you don't. You may even have seen your apparent physical problems, which may include stiffness in your back, shoulders raised while playing, tension in the waist down, or difficulty in handling certain technical challenges. You may also have perceived your emotional state while playing and even the quality of the sound.

The aim of this exercise is to raise your awareness of the fact that the way you play is the product of your specific ideas about your relationship with your instrument. In other words, you create your way of playing music through the idea you have of yourself as a musician—or the idea that others have about you as a musician, an idea that has been engraved in your subconscious mind. This is why the first step towards developing a way of playing that is free from all tension and filled with vibrant energy is to change the mental image you have of yourself as a player. You need to change your system of beliefs about your performance as a musician and to create a new mental program for your artistic development. In this way, the information flowing from your subconscious to your conscious mind will be clear and precise, and you will be able to achieve your objectives successfully.

How Do You See Yourself?

As discussed above, this study method requires internal changes in your view of yourself and your way of playing. At first it may seem like too much work, as you need to use all of your mental, emotional, and physical skills in your daily practice. However, over time, it will turn into a very effective internal strategy, which will make your practice a time of real progress and full of enjoyment in both technical and musical terms.

To conclude this chapter, let's go back to the last exercise. Try it again, but this time visualize yourself without any preconception. In other words, don't judge or criticize your way of playing; simply observe your performance. When you're finished, write down some notes about what you saw in your playing. The list might include some of the following:

- ➤ My neck is stiff when I play.
- ➤ I raise my shoulders when I change position.
- ➤ I move my arms too slowly.
- ➤ My tuning is slightly off.
- ➤ My sound is tight, which makes my body stiff.
- ➤ I get distracted while playing.

> ➤ I don't feel truly excited while playing.

On reflecting on the above, perhaps you will notice the similarity between your statements and your preconceived ideas about your way of playing, ideas resulting from your personal experience or from observations that other people have made about your playing, which you have internalized in such a way that they form part of your musical reality. All these ideas make up your system of beliefs, and it is precisely in this system that the changes need to happen.

As these are beliefs stored in your mind, it is in your mind where you can take the first step towards a new vision of yourself in terms of how you play your instrument.

To achieve this new vision, try the following exercise. Take some slow, deep breaths. Make a list of how you would like to see yourself playing, physically, emotionally, and mentally.

For example:

> ➤ My neck feels loose when I play.
> ➤ My shoulders are always down while I'm playing.
> ➤ My tuning is perfect.
> ➤ My sound flows and I enjoy playing.
> ➤ My concentration is excellent.
> ➤ My body feels free when I play.
> ➤ I experience specific emotions through my playing.
> ➤ I feel free while playing.

Once you've finished your list, visualize yourself in as much detail as possible playing your instrument exactly how you really want to play. Merely by thinking about it you will feel a sense of self-assurance and wellbeing. Of course, as noted previously, this is a process that takes time and dedication.

The purpose of the above exercises is to help you recognize that your playing is shaped by your beliefs about your playing. Once you have realized this and you start to replace those beliefs with others that foster creative and positive solutions, the results will be amazing. The key is that you will now be focusing on the solution rather than on the problem, and this makes a huge difference to the quality of your studying. This way of solving apparent problems will also sharpen your ability to listen to yourself and observe yourself while you practise—elements that are essential to successful studying. By developing your cognitive skills in this way, you will be able to play in a freer and more captivating way.

We have such an extraordinary wealth of information stored in our subconscious—memories of the past that have been piled up there without realizing it. The type of exercise proposed in this chapter can bring your deepest negative mindsets out into the open. In this way, you can replace them with new mindsets that are creative and positive.

Furthermore, being conscious of your apparent difficulties in playing your musical instrument will help you identify them more quickly and effectively. However, you should never focus on the problems, but always on the solutions. Progress in playing an instrument is often slowed down by the mental tendency to concentrate too much on our faults. The key here is to be conscious of what needs to be improved, while focusing at all times on the solution, on how you want to play the music. Stop talking about your problems with playing and turn your mind, discreetly, to your new goals as a musician. In this way, you'll start to break free of the bonds of the past and experience the world of sound in all its fullness.

It is important to be aware that it is normal for your mind, emotions, and body to resist this transformation at first. Be patient and persevere. Remember that you're strengthening a muscle that may have been lying dormant until now. This muscle is made up of your mental, emotional, and physical metacognitive powers, and by the unbreakable bond between them and the intention to create a new artist within.

Give yourself time for the change and take on the challenges on your musical journey in a healthy, creative, and enjoyable way. May every moment of your artistic creation be a call by your essence to express itself in a pure, powerful, and elevated way. Turn yourself into your own Michelangelo on each step of your artistic journey, a journey that will touch the hearts of your audiences.

SECTION 2:
PRACTICE

2.1. BODY BALANCE DURING PRACTICE

Everything, whether physical, mental or spiritual, is reflected in muscle tension.
(Alexander, quoted in Brennan,1994, p. 25)

The Alexander Technique

Before diving into the topic of this chapter, I would like to give a brief history of how the Alexander Technique was born. This technique was created by Frederick Matthias Alexander (1869-1955), an Australian actor. At a crucial moment in his career, Alexander began to suffer from problems with his voice when performing. He went to medical specialists to see what they could do for him. After some time, Alexander realized that the doctors could not solve his problem, and it was his own passion for acting and his desire to be completely cured that led him to create his own technique.

Alexander placed mirrors in strategic positions in his room, allowing him to see his body from different angles. Gradually he began to realize that if he put his body in a certain posture, he could project his voice with less effort. He thus began to develop specific exercises to achieve correct posture, which helped him not only cure himself so that he could act again, but also led him to become a therapist applying his own technique.

This is a compelling example of how human beings are capable of creating new ways of reaching their maximum capacity, a capacity that allows them to transform their apparent problems into strategies for both internal and external development. We all have a sage within us, ready to help us whenever we need them.

The Alexander Technique is an excellent method for reencountering your physical balance, as it can teach you how to use the exact level of physical energy you need for a musical performance. This is very important, because a lack of conscious contact with your body can lead you to exert more energy than is necessary when playing our musical instrument, which in turn creates unnecessary physical tension. This is why practising a method like this can prove highly beneficial to bring your physical condition up to its true state of total fitness. There are also other highly effective disciplines that help achieve a healthy and strong posture. Among these are the Feldenkrais Method, pilates, yoga, qigong, and Music and Movement. Everyone should seek out the discipline that suits them best: what matters is to be doing something to recover a healthy, strong, and flexible body.

The Effects of Modern Life on the Human Being

We live in an age in which so many changes are occurring at a breakneck pace. This can affect us in different ways in our everyday lives. We rush from one activity to the next, sometimes without even noticing, which leads to one of the most serious afflictions of our times: stress.

Constantly on the run, we have no time for reflection, as we place all our attention on the external world and allow it to rule our lives. The idea of stopping for a few minutes to be alone with ourselves and observe our feelings is unthinkable, as we cannot give ourselves the luxury of taking a few minutes a day; we simply do not have time.

This "no time to spare" is the mental slogan of the age in which we live. But if, as noted in previous chapters, every change needs to begin on the mental level, perhaps we need to start thinking that we really do have time, and to start spending a few minutes a day alone with ourselves, consciously relaxing our minds and bodies. These few minutes can make our everyday lives richer, more relaxed, and more harmonious.

Spending time with yourself can be hugely beneficial for you as a person and also as an artist, as the true art emerges from a space of total calm and from the power of silence.

For this and many other reasons, it is worth your while to foster consciousness of both body and mind. Start listening to your body and paying attention to the signals it sends. Thanks to these signals, you can get your body back to its natural state of full health and wellbeing. This state is the basis for an effective and sound technique.

Why do so many musicians suffer from physical tension? Why do so many musicians end up so tired, both physically and mentally, after a musical performance?

All of this exhaustion is caused by stress. When we're young, it isn't so obvious, because the natural physical condition of a child is generally relaxed and healthy. But as we grow up, we start to be affected by emotional and mental stress. This stress begins to cause physical tension in us and thus in our relationship with our instruments.

There are many things that can aggravate these tensions. One is the widespread idea that the more hours of study we do a day the better our results will be. Another is studying for hours without a break for physical relaxation, without realizing that musicians use their muscles the same way as athletes. There may also be mental and emotional issues that lead to all kinds of tensions in your body and, therefore, in your playing.

So how can we improve our bodily awareness in relation to music? To begin with, we need to change the idea that the more hours we study the better we'll play. This idea is valid up to a point, but we need to modify it to make the most of our daily practice.

To do this, we need to realize that it isn't the number of hours that will define how we play, but how effectively we manage the time to achieve good results. Becoming conscious of your body as a fundamental element of your practice will be a powerful strategy for changing the way you study, which will be greatly enhanced if you increase not the *quantity* of time but the *quality* of your practice in that time.

Another important step towards transforming your daily practice is to take conscious physical pauses, relaxing your body during the breaks you decide to establish during your musical-instrumental creative work time. As a result, instead of exhausting your aching muscles, you will complete your practice with a sensation of physical wellbeing.

Before focusing on how you can manage your physical condition during your daily practice, consider the differences between a tension-full and a tension-free body.

Science has determined the characteristics and reactions of a body in a state of stress and one in a state of complete wellbeing. The characteristics of a body in tension are:

- ➤ Improper management of respiration
- ➤ Exhaustion
- ➤ Muscular pain (ranging from mild to chronic)
- ➤ Nerves
- ➤ Mental stress
- ➤ Excessive effort in simple and complex physical actions
- ➤ Tense relationship with your musical instrument

The reactions of a body in tension are:

- ➤ Irritability
- ➤ Susceptibility to emotions like anger, fear, sadness, insecurity
- ➤ Weak immune system
- ➤ Reacting at the last minute
- ➤ Going from one action to the next without reflecting or allowing time for a pause between them

Conversely, the characteristics of a tension-free body are:

- ➤ Proper management of respiration
- ➤ Releasing your natural physical energy

➢ Toned muscles
➢ Ability to recognize tensions and release them consciously
➢ Conscious mental relaxation
➢ Development of a natural relationship with your instrument at the physical level

The reactions of a tension-free body are:
➢ High level of concentration on your daily activities
➢ Reflecting before acting
➢ Handling your emotions intelligently
➢ Trusting in your own capacities
➢ Strengthening your immune system
➢ Ease and effectiveness in your everyday activities
➢ Not seeking to control everything in your life; letting things flow

It is obvious that if we consider the characteristics of a body in tension and a body free of tension, a healthy, tension-free body would be preferable if you really want to feel good physically when playing your instrument and not end up with a lot of pain after performing.

Once you start to discover the benefits of a completely fit body, you will enjoy not only optimal health but also a richer experience when you play your instrument. In fact, certain technical challenges that once seemed impossible will become possible, as releasing your full physical and mental energy will help your body to react naturally to your instrument. The basis for achieving this is the intention that you adopt—the intention to change your way of playing and to see the world of music as a world that is found inside you and that resonates with everything around you.

Physical Preparation for Daily Practice

Preparing physically for your daily practice is essential if you want good results. With this in mind, try reflecting on the following questions:

How do you prepare for your practice normally?

Do you prepare your music and then immediately start playing?

Do you feel uptight at the start of your practice?

What is the space where you study like?

Do external situations interrupt your practice?

Write down the answers to these questions in your notebook. Make your answers as detailed as possible, especially with regard to physical aspects and external situations. Describe what your workspace is like and the external situations that are normally happening while you study.

Here's one possible (and all-too-common) daily practice scenario: you are stressed and tired from previous activities when you begin your practice; emotionally you may be feeling anger, frustration, fear, or apathy caused by some situation prior to your practice; mentally you may feel confused because you don't know what you want to achieve in your practice, you only know that you've got to study. To better describe the above, consider the example of an internal monologue that might be running through your mind before you start practising:

"As soon as I finish what I'm doing now I'm going to start studying. I have to hurry to allow time to study the piece. I have to get started as quickly as possible" (this unleashes a feeling of anxiety) "I hope I can play it better today. I practice it and practice it, but I don't feel like I'm making any progress with this piece" (this provokes a feeling of frustration).

And now you prepare your instrument, the music, the stand, and you start studying in this frame of mind.

This is just one example of how many of us start our daily practice. There are, of course, many other possibilities. What is important here is that you become aware of the fact that your practice will depend totally on how you approach it, i.e., the attitude you have towards your daily study. Most probably, the result of approaching your practice in the way described in the above example would be an anxious, apathetic, and aimless study session. If you're already tense when you start studying, you'll become even tenser as you practice.

With this kind of result, merely thinking about studying will obviously start to provoke a feeling of rejection of your musical instrument, as studying will mean having to face a lot of physical, emotional, and mental issues related to your personal and musical identity. It is a question of creating a new system of beliefs about your work with your instrument and creating a new artistic identity.

So, what can you do to change this attitude towards studying? What steps can you take to turn it into an enjoyable moment that you are fully present for?

What you could do is to become more aware of your body and transform all the physical aspects of your daily practice into something positive in order to achieve the best results.

To achieve this kind of awareness, it is important to change your physical approach to studying. By "physical" I mean not only the state of your body but also all the external factors that can influence the results of your practice. These factors can include: the space where you study, the time of day, the people who are normally around at the time, and the devices that might be within your reach.

It is advisable to find a space where your practice can be a harmonious experience, as the nature of your environment will influence your mind and emotions while you're studying.

As far as the time of your practice is concerned, you need to be receptive to be able to find the time when you feel that you perform most effectively. You may not always be able to practice at the same time every day, but it is important to try and respect the schedule you decide on.

What is essential is to maintain an enthusiastic discipline in relation to your daily practice. To do this, you need to work out what your priorities are and to stick to them, as to successfully achieve a specific goal, intelligent persistence is the key.

The people around us are also an important influence. There are people in your life who understand the importance of music practice and others who do not. It is essential to ask the people around you not to interrupt you while you are practising, unless it is a real emergency. If you respect your internal space and your priorities, others will, too. The more focused you are in your practice, the more you will get out of it. On the other hand, if you are unfocused, the time you set aside for practice will seem to slip through your hands.

Mechanical devices can also affect your study. Telephones, televisions, computers, and cell phones should be kept out of your practice space. How often does your phone ring while you're practising, and you pick it up without giving it a second thought? This immediately cuts the focused energy you need to build up while studying. Recovering this energy after the interruption will require twice the effort. It is also important not to make phone calls during breaks in your study, watch television, use the computer, or check social media. These activities cut the energy you have created in your practice.

This is why it is important not to get distracted while studying, because if you do, on the neural level you will drop out of an alpha state and into a beta state, where your analytical mind (focused on ideas or mental conversations unrelated to your study) will take over.

As noted above, it is absolutely vital to establish a positive attitude towards your instrument practice. Seeing it as a moment of profound contact with the music and with your own being will help you start enjoying your daily practice and start getting the best results out of it. Ultimately, the mission of music is to enrich our lives every time we enter that wonderful world of sound that resonates within us.

2.2. PHYSICAL PREPARATION FOR INSTRUMENT PRACTICE

It is important for you to become more conscious of your physical wellbeing in relation to your musical instrument, and of the environment where you practise every day. If you are suffering from physical tension, this will have a negative impact on your playing. External situations on your music practice and the frame of mind with which you approach your practice will also have an effect on your progress. Reflecting on all these considerations may help you identify different possibilities for improving your performance when studying and enjoying your practice to the fullest.

One of these possibilities is keeping yourself in good physical condition for your study by engaging in physical exercise. To this end, it's a good idea to have a yoga mat or quilted blanket on hand, as it will be of use for certain exercises that can prepare you for your daily practice.

The goals of these exercises are:

1. To make you aware of the importance of physical wellbeing as a basis for an effective technique and expressive musicality.
2. To foster an awareness of your own body so that you view yourself as a musical athlete.
3. To carry out physical exercises before, during, and after each practice.
4. To create a tension-free physical relationship with your instrument.
5. To learn to listen to your body before, during, and after your daily practice.
6. To connect the need for expression to the playing action that accurately and naturally represents it.

Before beginning these exercises, prepare the space for your musical creativity (you could try referring to your practice with this or a similar term if you wish). Carry out a visual motor rehearsal, where your mind feels the sensation of physical wellbeing that you want to achieve through the exercises. This mental guidance will enable you to relax and tone your muscles more effectively.

Lay your mat on the floor. Take your shoes off. Now that the space is ready, carry out the following physical exercises:

1. Lie face-up on the mat, with the palms of your hands also facing upwards. Keep your neck from arching, ensuring that it is in line with your back. To do this, bring your chin down towards your breastbone so

91

that you can feel a straight line from your back to your neck. If necessary, place a small, folded towel under your head to keep your neck straight.

2. Let the full weight of your body relax on the floor. Release all the tension in every muscle.

3. Take some abdominal breaths. Inhale for four beats and then exhale for four beats. Pause for four seconds between each inhalation and exhalation. On each exhalation, try to expel all the tension built up in your body, while letting out an "ahhh".

4. Work your way through your body, focusing on relaxing each part of it, starting with your feet, and ending with the top of your head. It often helps to place your hand over your abdomen to help you focus your attention on your breathing.

5. Concentrate on the energy all around your body. Start at your feet and work your way up to your head.

6. Cross your hands and place them over your chest. Perform the Quick Coherence® technique.

7. Stretch your arms slowly back while stretching your feet out. After a few seconds, bring your arms back to their original position and relax your feet. Carry out this step several times.

8. Turn slowly to your right and adopt the fetal position; then push yourself up with your left hand into a crouching posture.

9. Move from this position onto a chair with your back straight and your feet firmly on the floor. Press your right nostril closed with your thumb, inhale slowly through your left nostril for four beats, then cover the left nostril with your finger and exhale through your right nostril. Perform this sequence eight times.

10. Place your hands on your thighs and take a few deep breaths while focusing your attention on your abdomen, releasing all thoughts from your mind.

11. In your seated position in the chair, stretch your neck slowly. While keeping your back straight, turn your neck slowly to the right and take a few breaths, while imagining your neck relaxing. Then turn to the right and do the same. Return to the middle and slowly lower your head forwards towards your breastbone, breathing deeply and focusing on relaxing your neck. Return slowly to your original position. It is important to keep your back straight during this stretch, which is designed to release all the tensions built up in your neck.

12. Stand up and compare how your body feels now with how you felt before the physical exercises. Let all your weight fall towards your feet and observe the good feeling caused by your conscious relaxation while breathing slowly and deeply.

13. Make slow circular movements with your shoulders, arms, hips, legs, and feet.
14. Extend your right arm and pull your right wrist downward gently with your left hand. Do the same with your left arm and right hand.
15. Now sit down again with your back straight. Take a three-pound weight in each hand while looking straight ahead (do not squeeze the weights in your hands; take them freely with only as much force as you need for this exercise). Lift each weight eight times, switching between one arm and the other. It is important to inhale first and exhale upon lifting the weight. Perform the same sequence again. This exercise can be optional.
16. Walk around the room looking straight ahead and loosening up your body on each step. After a few steps, walk around in a playing position, but without your instrument.

It is just as important to tone your body before studying as it is to establish a free physical relationship with your musical instrument. With this in mind, try the following activities, which can be carried out after completing the ones described above. The activities are:

1. Pick up your instrument and take a few slow, deep breaths.
2. Walk around the space while playing a few long notes and breathing slowly and deeply with your abdomen at the same time.
3. Play a passage of a piece you are currently working on, placing all your attention on your abdominal breathing. When you finish, put your instrument down on a chair.
4. Using a simple choreographed set of movements, approach your instrument, pick it up and place it in a playing position.
5. With your instrument in hand, turn your torso slowly to the right and then to the left. Repeat this sequence six times.
6. Walk in the space with your instrument and perform a simple choreographed set of movements with it, without playing.
7. Play a scale while bending and stretching your knees on each note you play.
8. Choose a passage of a piece you are working on. Play it while walking around the room.
9. Play the same passage while performing a simple choreographed set of movements.

Performing these music and movement exercises will help tone your body and make your muscles more flexible. This will be of great benefit to your technique, because the looser your body is, the easier it will be for you to tackle technical and musical challenges. At the same time, it will enhance your physical relationship with your musical instrument. Think of yourself in this exercise as a dancer.

Intention is key to physical toning prior to study. This means that you need to be clear in your mind that your intention in these physical activities is to relax and tone your body. Without a clear intention, your mind will begin to wander onto other topics, which will reduce the effectiveness of the exercises as you would be performing them mechanically. But when your intention is clear, your mind will be present in the action of relaxing and toning your body. This will help you achieve very positive results and you will realize that strengthening your body is the basis for a solid and effective technique that will enable you to express yourself as an artist more powerfully.

2.3. BODY AWARENESS DURING AND AFTER PRACTICE

It is as important to prepare yourself physically before your study time as it is to maintain a good physical condition while practising. Even if you have prepared physically for your practice, it is important to take some breaks for physical relaxation to keep your muscles from contracting. As noted earlier, musicians use all their muscles just like athletes do, although it is not so noticeable, because normally a musician stands or sits in the same position and doesn't move around like an athlete.

Try the following activities to keep your body in good condition during your daily practice:

1. During your study, make circular movements with your legs, shoulders, hips, and arms, followed by a deep breath. Finish this activity by walking around the space.
2. While lying on a yoga mat, stretch your arms back and stretch the tips of your toes downward. Return to your original position and repeat this sequence eight times. Inhale and exhale while stretching.
3. Scan your body from head to toe, placing your attention in the energy around each part of your body.
4. Observe and perceive your physical condition throughout your practice time. The moment you feel any tension or pain, put your instrument down and do some of the physical exercises you use to prepare for practice. Always do them consciously, i.e., with the intention of relaxing the part of your body where you feel the tension.
5. While standing up straight, inhale and exhale letting out the sound "ahhhh!" This will relax you emotionally and physically.
6. Take note of your posture. For example, if you have a tendency to curve your back or lift your shoulders when you play, try to return them to their normal position every time you notice this. In this way, your instrument will begin adapting to your body and not the other way around, and you will be conditioning your body to play free of tensions.
7. Before correcting your posture or relaxing your body, imagine yourself relaxed and with the right posture that you want to have when holding your instrument. For example, if you tend to raise your shoulders while playing, imagine yourself with your shoulders relaxed. By directing your corrections with your mind, you will make them more effective because you will be doing it with the power of your intention.
8. During your practice breaks, do any of the preparatory exercises described above.

9. Breathe through your abdomen all the time. This will keep your energy flowing constantly, as when you breathe properly, your energy circulates, but when you forget to breathe, the energy begins to get blocked. Whenever you breathe, always do it slowly and in a relaxed manner.

10. When you've finished your practice, lie down back on your mat. Stretch your arms slowly up over your head and stretch the tips of your toes down. When you bring your arms back to their original position, contract the tips of your toes. Do this several times.

11. Upon completing these movements, inhale, and exhale deeply. Feel your body thanking you for how you are treating it. When you're ready, lift yourself up on one side and get into a crouching position with your back bent down over your legs and your arms down at your sides.

12. Take a few breaths and raise your spinal column slowly to an upright position, one vertebra at a time. When you're ready, raise your right knee, support yourself on your right leg and stand up, keeping your back straight as you do.

13. Place your hands on your abdomen once more, thanking your body for being an excellent instrument for your musical expression.

The purpose of these activities is to keep your body in good condition so that it can play a positive role in your playing, rather than being one more obstacle to the fulfilment of your potential as a performer.

Recognizing your body's condition as the basis for a solid playing technique will help you discover your true abilities. For example, if you find that a particular technical challenge, such as a change of position, is extremely difficult, it is probably due to a large extent to physical tensions. Changing position while your shoulders are hunched and tense is not the same as doing it with your shoulders relaxed. Once such tensions are released, your body will begin to respond naturally and amazingly.

Now, I want to highlight four key factors for a successful relationship between your body consciousness and your work as a musician. These four factors are: breathing, the use of your mind, the position of your jaw, and your consciousness of heart coherence while playing.

Breathing

The idea of breathing continuously through your abdomen may seem strange at first, as it is a question that is rarely addressed in music teaching. Musical pedagogy does include the idea of breathing, but generally it involves breathing through the lungs, and only at the beginning of a piece. The rest of the time, it is mostly a forgotten topic. However, breathing through the lungs tends to be quite limited in terms of the amount of oxygen our body receives, while abdominal breathing, being deeper, is more effective in this respect. This is why it is important to be patient and persistent when integrating this new element into your playing.

With perseverance, you will start noticing the benefits of this method. These benefits include: fewer muscle tensions when playing, as you will be constantly sending oxygen to every part of your body; better concentration, because thanks to the connection between abdomen and brain, this kind of breathing will relax your mind and enhance its capacity; and greater confidence and self-assurance in relation to your playing.

To integrate this form of breathing into your playing, it is recommended to begin using it consciously in very simple technical exercises like the preparatory activities described above. In this way, you will focus on your breathing and not on the difficulty of the exercise. The key is to turn it into a habit. And like any habit, it will take time to become a natural part of your relationship with the world of sound and with your musical instrument.

In this respect, it is worth considering singers, who use this kind of breathing, as you can learn a lot from their approach to breathing and how this influences the tone and depth of their voices, as we are expressing our voice through our playing.

The Mind

The second key factor for body consciousness is being as mentally focused as possible to ensure best results. Mental focus is used by athletes who always visualize their routines before competing. What they are doing is preparing their body on the mental level so that it will respond optimally during the competition. In the same way, if you have a clear mental intention to tone and relax your body before each practice, your body will respond with genuinely profound and alert relaxation.

To achieve this, it is advisable, before beginning your physical preparation for studying, to imagine yourself in a relaxed and toned physical state. This will give your mind a clear sense of what you want to achieve through the physical exercises, so that the results manifest more clearly on the physical level.

If you have a tendency to begin studying with stiffness in your legs or shoulders, imagine them relaxed and toned before beginning the sequence of physical exercises. Carrying out a preparatory relaxation sequence in a mechanical way is very different from doing it consciously. The intention to achieve good physical condition is essential to ensure that the physical exercises really benefit your performance as a musician.

The Jaw

The optimal function of your jaw is another key factor for effective playing. You are probably usually aware of your arms, legs, hips, neck, and shoulders, and the importance of keeping them tension-free. But in the music world, very little attention is given to the jaw. It might seem like a very small part of your body, and yet it is extraordinary how much tension can build up in it. This stiffness is often provoked by emotions like frustration or anger. It is a subtle tension, but one that can accumulate over time until it starts affecting your whole body. A stiff jaw can stiffen your whole occipital zone, the region around the base of the skull. This in turn can provoke tension in your neck, shoulders, and upper back. For this reason, consciously relaxing your jaw can be of great help in the process of eliminating physical tensions. It is interesting to observe how small children, when they are tackling a difficult task, tend to open their mouths, as if their natural instinct is to slacken their jaws to make the task easier. It may look kind of funny, but it really is an intelligent and effective response to that situation.

One way of relaxing your jaw is by getting into a relaxed position on the floor, taking a few deep breaths, and opening your mouth until you feel your jaw slackening. Usually, you don't need to open your mouth that wide. This exercise can be done as part of your preparatory exercises prior to studying.

Another effective method is consciously relaxing your jaw while playing. To do this you need to open your mouth, recall the sensation of relaxation, and then after a moment close your mouth again, or leave it open if you feel it necessary at that time. In this way, you will be ensuring a tension-free jaw. It is like opening a physical and emotional padlock, as this is a part of the body that tends to capture built-up emotions, both past and present.

It is so important to think of your body as the foundation for a solid and natural performance. Conscious relaxation and toning of your body constitute a powerful method for opening the door to a way of playing your instrument that is completely free of tension. Constant application of this new approach to playing will help you foster a positive relationship with your instrument. You and your instrument can then form a single unit through which the power of the music can flow unimpeded. Think of your body as an extension of your ideas and of your heart. Every physical movement you make should not be merely a mechanical action but an impulse responding to your need for the most powerful expression.

Heart Coherence while Playing Your Instrument

Inside your heart is an infinite creative power. But you may not always be aware of this or be able to access that power.

To achieve a true connection with the music you are playing, it is essential first of all to come into direct contact with yourself through the energy of your heart. Once you have achieved this contact, your body will react much more naturally and will become a perfect medium for the expression of your musical ideas. In this way, you can make contact firstly with your own essence, and then with the essence of the world of sound.

It has been scientifically proven that coherent energy in our hearts affects our brains, thereby establishing a harmonious relationship between the two. For thirty years, the HeartMath Institute in Boulder Creek, California, has been conducting research on heart intelligence.

For your musical performances, there is a simple activity you can carry out to help you feel and understand that your heart is connected to your brain and how this connection can greatly enhance your playing.

The activity is as follows:

1. Cross your hands over the centre of your chest and perform the Quick Coherence ® technique.
2. Bring to your mind a passage of a piece you are working on. While visualizing it, keep your hands crossed over the middle of your chest.
3. Take your instrument in your hands and play the same passage, putting all your attention on the energy emanating from the middle of your heart
4. Write down your reflections.

The activity described above will guide you to start making contact with the immense power in your heart. The third part of this book discusses in detail the importance of generating heart coherence and its impact on your playing. It is the power of your heart that emanates from you in every live performance.

To play an instrument, you need your mind, heart, and fingertips... (Anonymous)

2.4. THE CREATIVE POWER OF THE MIND DURING INSTRUMENT PRACTICE

> Every technical or musical problem is resolved first at the mental level. (Derbez, 2015)

This chapter explores the huge potential we have in our minds and how we can apply it creatively in our daily practice through our metacognitive capacities. This potential within us is something that we often tend to ignore because we generally want to solve problems from the outside in rather than from the inside out. Yet you can achieve much more if you tackle every challenge you face in your practice on the mental level first.

Before beginning your physical preparation for each study, you can use your mental capacity to imagine your physical wellbeing. In other words, before relaxing your body, you can direct your mental intention with images and thoughts like: "I relax my mind and my body now." In this way, you are meeting a challenge based on an internal intention which, in this particular case, will relax you consciously rather than just mechanically. This is the very core message of this new vision of music: meeting every challenge in your daily practice through your own inner drive. In this way, you will be bringing your true qualities to your practice.

Let me give you an example of how we tend to try to deal with a problem from the outside in. During my time in Lugano, one of my teachers worked exclusively on my technique for the first six months. My technique definitely improved; the only problem was that the approach to correcting my technique during those six months was external, as the teacher focused on correcting my positioning with precise physical movements of my fingers and hands, which thus became mechanical, rather than using my mental intention to correct myself. As a result, after these months of technique, other problems that existed before that period reemerged. It was the reemergence of those problems that got me thinking about a new way of studying a musical instrument and of perceiving the world of sound, as well as a new approach to music method.

It is very common in music teaching to try to solve problems exclusively on a physical level. But this causes so many physical, emotional, and mental tensions in advanced music students, and even in professional musicians.

The Importance of your Mental State in Your Daily Practice

In the previous chapter, I asked you to reflect on your physical state when you begin your daily practice. Now, I would like to invite you to do the same for your mental state. Ask yourself the following questions:

Are you clear about what and how you are going to study before you start playing?

What are you thinking about before and during your practice?

Do you know what your goals are for each study session?

Do you know what kind of sound you want to express through your musical instrument?

Do you know the direction you want to take your practice?

Is your mind in a beta state or an alpha state?

Is your heart coherent or incoherent?

Write down the answers that come to your mind spontaneously.

Many of us begin our daily practice without knowing exactly what we're going to study, how we're going to study it or, most importantly, what our goals are for the practice session. We walk in, pick up our musical instrument, and start playing right away. The lack of a plan for your practice can result in confusion, distraction and even frustration. Think of yourself as a musical architect. You need a visual plan and an effective strategy to make real progress in each practice.

Before going into detail about how to use your mental potential in your practice and how to make a plan for it, I'd like to point out a very common mistake made in music practice: constant repetition without reflecting on the reason behind the repetition.

This situation arises because you are repeating a passage over and over without knowing exactly what it is that you want to improve with each repetition. Repetition isn't the problem; the problem is doing it without reflecting, without establishing a clear intention before each repetition using your metacognitive capacities. In this way you create physical tension, because you get frustrated by the lack of improvement in the passage you're studying, and your muscles start to tighten up. To transform this repetition in a healthy way, think of yourself as a painter of sounds. A painter doesn't just paint the whole painting without stopping. She applies a brush stroke, looks at it, reflects on what she wants to see and express on the canvas, and then applies the next stroke. Similarly, repetition can become conscious and creative if you apply your whole being to it—mind, body, and emotions.

Now that I've highlighted the importance of having a mental plan for each practice session and using your metacognitive capacities while studying, I invite you to try the following strategies, which can greatly increase the quality of your practice and your playing in general.

Once you've prepared the space and your body for your practice, make a plan for the session. This plan, which may be mental or written, should:

1. State exactly what you are going to study and how much time you will spend on each section of your practice.
2. State what aspect of your playing you want to improve in that session.
3. In terms of technique, clarify the goals that you want to achieve in the session with the passage or technical element so that it can support an authentic expression.
4. In terms of pieces of music, identify the type of sound and phrasing you want to express in the piece and the technical agility you want to achieve in it.
5. Define the level of expression you want to achieve as it is important to have a clear goal beforehand in order to direct your intention creatively in each practice.
6. Establish your break times. To this end, it is important to observe how you feel during your practice, as this will determine the physical or mental exercises you should do during the breaks to enhance the quality of your practice.

And of course, the key ingredient, the underlying strategy in your practice, is to follow this plan consciously, i.e., using your mental metacognitive skills at all times in your practice. Every objective needs to be visualized in your mind before you physically carry it out, as this will ensure your actions are as sound and precise as possible.

Below is an example of the kind of study plan described in the previous paragraphs:

Study Plan (Example)

1. Today I will study the C major scale and the Bach piece I've been working on. I have seventy minutes for my practice today. I will devote ten minutes to physical preparation, five minutes to meditation, fifteen minutes to the scale and thirty-five minutes to Bach. The remaining five minutes will be for a break and a heart coherence exercise.
2. Today I will work on my tuning and create a fuller and deeper sound.
3. By practising this scale, I will enhance my tuning and my changes of position will become swifter and more precise. I will ensure that I play the scale expressively.

4. My goal with this Bach piece is to perform it with a dynamic force that will allow the audience to perceive the specific range of emotions I want to express in this piece. To do this, today I will create a more expansive and powerful sound with close attention to the specific phrasing I am aiming for in the piece. I will also observe the agility and precision of my technique so that it meets my expressive needs effectively. I will feel the emotions I want to express through Bach. [Try visualizing the sound and phrasing of the piece in a position in which you feel your level of concentration is at its best. This may be while sitting in a chair or squatting with your back straight or on your mat.]

5. During my break I will do some abdominal breathing and stretches with the intention of relaxing and toning my body and ensuring heart coherence.

A specific study plan like this is very effective because when you know exactly what you're going to study and what your goals are, your mind will be clearly and precisely focused, and as a result your actions will likewise be clear and precise. You will thus be directing your intention, creatively and consciously, towards your goal as an artist and a performer.

Your study plan should always be expressed in the first person. The use of the first person in this way is part of a learning method known as self-correction. Self-correction is a highly effective element in this new way of studying music. Later in this chapter I will explain this strategy in more detail, and how it applies to music practice. It is all about establishing a new system of belief.

Mental Focus in Your Daily Practice

So far, we've looked at the importance of knowing what you want from your daily study sessions. Now, let's consider another essential part of a successful music practice: how to work during your practice.

Once again, think of yourself as a painter of sounds. Just as the painter reflects on her work before applying the next brush stroke, musicians need to reflect and observe to give their practice meaning and intention. If you consider your work as a musician in this way, you will gradually eliminate the common habit of repetition for its own sake, as it can often cause confusion and even create feelings of frustration and anger when it fails to produce any noticeable progress in our practice. According to traditional Chinese medicine, frustration and anger are emotions that affect the liver, which is the organ that regulates the tendons. They can thus give rise to physical conditions like tendinitis.

This is why it is important to be very attentive to the emotions you feel while practising, as they have a profound influence on your physical condition. As discussed in the first part of this book, negative emotions can release cortisol into your body, which in the long term can create a lot of physical tension that will in turn affect your playing. This does not mean that you should deny such negative emotions; instead, simply observe them and determine at that moment to replace them with positive emotions like calm and joy.

Knowing exactly what you want to achieve in your daily practice is already a big step forward towards conscious repetition, as you already have your goals in mind beforehand. This approach will even enhance your capacity for observation and listening as your ears will know what they should be listening for. In other words, by having in mind what you want to get out of your music practice, you will be guiding your hearing to "observe" that your actual playing matches your mental image of the music. The mind-hearing-perception bond can turn you into your own best teacher.

This bond will guide you in terms of how to study during your music practice. In addition, for this guidance to be completely successful, you will need to listen both to the quality of sound you are producing and to your emotional responses while playing. It is also essential to observe that your physical actions match your mental and emotional intentions. All of this will provide a framework for making conscious repetitions with the objective of improving with each repetition; but to do this you need to know what it is you're trying to correct.

Before going into detail about how to study, take a moment to reflect on how you see yourself as an artist.

Perhaps the answer that comes to your mind is something like: "I'm a musician, a creator of sounds," or "I'm a performer, as I perform a work written by a composer," or perhaps "as a musician I present a composition so that an audience can appreciate it." All of this means you are a creative being—an artist on multiple levels. You are an actor, because you express a character through the music; you are a painter, because you draw colours and images with sounds; and you are a dancer, because you use your whole body to bring out the world of sound around you and in your heart. Seeing yourself as the multifaceted artist you truly are will help you create a work of art every time you are in contact with your instrument and with the music.

Mental Metacognitive Strategies for Daily Practice

The mental metacognitive activities proposed for your daily practice have the following objectives:

1. Transformation on the mental level as a performer.
2. Incorporation of visualization to resolve technical and expressive issues.
3. Application of a mental sound map in daily practice.

4. Use of the visual motor rehearsal technique for the development of conscious repetition.
5. Incorporation of self-correction into daily practice.
6. Mental self-perception during daily music practice.
7. Development of metacognitive awareness.
8. Application of meditation as a way of preparing the brain waves necessary for a successful practice.
9. Development of a harmonic heart to establish mental coherence.

Try the following activities to develop the ability to practice while using your mental metacognitive powers to the maximum. The activities are split into three separate parts.

Part A:

1. Choose a piece you are currently studying.
2. Make a study plan and write it down.
3. Take some slow, deep breaths to bring your mind into an alpha state of relaxation.
4. Carry out a series of physical exercises (see the chapter on physical preparation prior to practice).
5. Place your hands across your chest and perform the Quick Coherence* technique, as follows:

Step 1. Focus your attention on the area of the heart. Imagine your breath is flowing in and out of your heart or chest area, breathing a little slower and deeper than usual. Find an easy rhythm that is comfortable.

Step 2. As you continue heart-focused breathing, make a sincere attempt to experience a regenerative feeling such as appreciation or care for someone or something in your life.

6. Make a precise mental sound map of the whole piece (phrasing, dynamics, sonority, emotional intention).
7. Place your hands across your chest and perform the Quick Coherence* technique again.
8. Visualize yourself playing the piece at least three times, as you would like to play it. Place your hands over your heart again during this step.
9. Play the piece.
10. In a notebook, write down all the positive aspects of your performance.

11. Write all the aspects of your performance that you feel you could improve. Write down these aspects in the first person. For example: My phrasing of the first passage is clear and expressive. My tuning is excellent throughout the piece.

The activities described above will give you a general map of the piece you are studying so that you can establish a clear and precise goal.

Part B:

1. Divide the piece into specific sections.
2. Choose one of these sections. Take some slow, deep breaths to bring your mind into an alpha state of relaxation and creativity.
3. Make a mental sound map of the section three times, while placing your attention on the centre of your heart.
4. Perform a visual motor rehearsal of the section three times. In this mental rehearsal, keep a clear idea of your phrasing, sonority, dynamics, physical movement, and the emotion you want to express through the section. Imagine yourself playing freely.
5. Play the passage.
6. When you finish playing, decide what you want to improve in the next run-through. For example, if you want to improve the tuning, imagine this in your mind. Imagine your fingers falling on the right place for a perfect, clear tuning. Once you're done, play the section again.

The last step will vary depending on what you want to improve. For example:

1. If you want to improve the **phrasing**, clarify in your mind again the musical direction you want to give the part you are studying; in other words, keep a clear idea of the key notes in the phrase and how you want to play them. Perform a simple set of movements with your body to represent the phrase. Once you have this clear, your body movements will correspond naturally to your musical intention. You will be able to see this in your next conscious repetition of the section.
2. If you want to improve your **sound**, decide exactly what kind of sound you want to produce in the section you're studying. Before repeating the passage, imagine this sound by associating it with an element of nature. For example, if you want to play a very delicate *pianissimo*, imagine the sound quality that you want to achieve in your mind and at the same time picture a far-off mist or a gentle wind sweeping along the autumn leaves.

This will help you internalize the sound of the passage so that you can play it more naturally in the next repetition.

3. If you want to improve the **dynamics**, use the same guide described above for the activity above.

4. If you want to improve the **rhythm** of the passage you're studying, imagine the rhythm until you feel you can hear the rhythm clearly in your mind. You can also try walking in step to this rhythm or playing it out with a percussion instrument. By doing this, you will be internalizing the rhythm just as you did with the sound so that you will be able to emanate it clearly and expressively.

5. If what you want to improve is a **technical** element of the piece, imagine yourself doing it exactly and effectively before repeating. For example, if while playing you noticed that you changed your elbow position too slowly and that this affected the sound you were aiming for, imagine yourself playing the part with a swift and precise elbow movement. At the same time, feel the emotion that you want to express. In this way, you will be guiding your body effectively through your conscious intention.

6. If you want to improve your **physical** sensation when playing the passage you're studying, conjure up in your mind the physical condition you need to play it and take some slow, deep, abdominal breaths. Once you've done this, imagine yourself free of tensions as you play with a feeling of plenitude, placing your attention on the centre of your heart. Now play the section again, focusing on your breath. While practising it's a good idea to keep reminding your body of its physical wellbeing, which is essential for an effective musical performance.

7. If you want to improve the **transitions** between phrases, clarify in your mind exactly how you want to play them and where you will breathe within them.

8. After working on the piece in sections, visualize your mental sound map of the whole piece again, feeling the full range of emotions that you want to express while playing it.

Part C:

1. Visualize yourself playing the piece. You may wish to imagine playing it on a stage, performing wonderfully with a sound and expressiveness that fills the space. Keep your attention on the centre of your heart while you are visualizing.

2. Play the piece again.

3. Write down your observations in relation to the differences between your first performance of the piece and this last one.

Part C of this study process can be completed after a few days of working on the piece in sections. The most important thing is to have a point of reference with Part A to observe everything that has improved throughout this process where you're using your mental metacognitive skills.

It is a good idea to take a break between each part. During these breaks, you can do some relaxation or meditation exercises. The importance of meditation for daily music practice is discussed later in this book.

The activities described above will create a healthy and creative attitude towards your music practice. In this sense, it is very important to learn to stop judging yourself for apparent mistakes you make while practising. In other words, don't judge yourself while playing, as this can block your thoughts and emotions. Instead, simply observe yourself and do conscious repetitions, thereby encouraging the development of your true metacognitive skills. Always remember to repeat passages in a conscious and focused way and to observe yourself throughout your practice, so that you are always clear on why you are repeating them. Before each repetition think first what you did very well and then what you could improve. In this way, you will be turning your practice time into a time of artistic creativity rather than a mere obligatory chore. You can also change your use of language, using the word "process" instead of "mistake"; in this way, you can relax and stop judging yourself, recognizing that everything that happens in your practice is simply part of the creative process.

Finally, it is important to remember to place your attention on the centre of your heart while carrying out a visual motor rehearsal or playing a piece. This is because by breathing from the centre of your heart while playing or visualizing, you will bring your heart into coherence, automatically silencing the obstructions of your analytical mind, and your brain will become more coherent. Your brain waves will shift from beta to alpha and your body will respond better to the goals you have set for the piece.

Self-correction

It takes time to internalize all the elements described above so that they become normal study habits. The results may not be obvious or palpable at first, but with commitment and dedication you will start to see the results and will be amazed by them.

This method of co-creation with the music will have you making use of the bond between mind, emotions, and body. This bond could be described as a muscle, and like any muscle, it needs exercise for it to work fully and effectively. This is why you need to be patient and believe in your true personal and artistic capacities. It is also important to always do the best you can in each practice, consciously employing all the strategies outlined in this book, along with others you find on your never-ending musical journey.

One technique that is vital to this new vision of practising an instrument is self-correction. This technique consists of correcting yourself aloud, using the present tense and the first person. It is a powerful strategy that will help you achieve what you're aiming for more quickly and effectively. After trying out this technique, one student of mine commented that it "works like magic!" Self-correction helps consolidate your intention to play your musical instrument just as you've been imagining during the study process.

Correcting yourself aloud in the first person intensifies the mind-body relationship. One clear example of this is the mental attitude of athletes, who set themselves a goal before each competition, and hold thoughts in their minds like: "I achieve the goal successfully" or "I run an excellent race today." In this way, athletes use their power of determination through self-correction, which contains within it the intention referred to above. And it is precisely this intention that can help you achieve your goals as an artist.

So how do you use this technique, and when should you use it? The use of self-correction at just the right moment will help you to bring every musical process you visualize mentally into reality. Self-correction can be used before or after your mental planning for your practice. To get a clearer idea of this concept, try the following exercise:

1. Choose a passage from the piece you are studying.
2. Determine what aspect of your playing of the passage you want to improve.
3. Imagine the passage as you would like to play a few times. For example, if you want to improve your sound quality, imagine yourself playing the passage with the sound that you would like to achieve with your instrument.
4. If what you want is a deeper and more expressive sound, say the following aloud to yourself: "I achieve a rich depth of sound in this passage. I emanate an expressive and vibrant sound quality." Repeat these phrases several times.
5. Play the passage.
6. Write your reflections on this exercise in your notebook.

Self-correction also requires some time and practice for its results to become evident, but these can often appear sooner than you expect. It all depends on your attitude towards self-correction itself. If you apply this technique mechanically, it will not be very effective. But if you use it with genuine conviction, your level of playing will improve noticeably, and you will be amazed by the positive results that self-correction can produce.

When using self-correction, it is advisable to pronounce each word slowly and clearly, as in this way your mind will be genuinely focused on your intention. Your ears will also be more alert as you will be more consciously aware of exactly what it is that you want to hear. In other words, you will be guided by your own conscious intention through the technique of self-correction.

It is important to remember that self-correction is only a support for the other techniques you use in your practice. Under no circumstances can it substitute the other elements of the study process.

Appendix B provides some sample phrases for this concept of self-correction. These phrases are intended to support technical and expressive elements in the study process.

One activity that can take self-correction to a deeper level is remembering your self-correction phrases just before you go to sleep. At that moment, your brain is generating melatonin and your brain waves are in alpha or theta. It is in this mental state that the changes can occur in your subconscious, which, as mentioned above, regulates your physiological reactions, and it is there that the transformation of your system of beliefs will really take place.

The Art of Phrasing in the Preparation of a Piece of Music

The process of preparing a piece of music is itself an art. You need to have a lot of patience and love for the beauty of the piece to achieve your best performance. One of the most complex elements in this process is the phrasing, i.e., how we want to shape the series of sounds in a piece of music.

The first time I heard the word "phrasing" was when I began studying in Switzerland. Until then, I was not aware of the importance of having a clear concept of a musical phrase. However, over the course of my career as a music teacher I have realized that the subtle question of how to tackle a phrase is extremely important for a student's learning process. The clearer you are about the details of how to create a phrase, the more enriching your musical performance will be.

The search for a clear and expressive phrasing is a process of indescribable beauty. Identifying the key notes of a phrase, how to reach them, the breaths between notes, the invisible space between notes, and the different sonorities that can be played all form part of the wondrous complexity of the art of phrasing. Understanding phrasing can be compared to a sculptor's ability to turn the materials they work with to express their artistic creations.

To apply this idea, try the following activities.

1. Choose a phrase in a piece you are studying.
2. Identify the key notes of the phrase.
3. Clarify in your mind the direction you want to give the phrase and how you want to direct the notes towards the key notes.
4. Based on the emotion you want to emanate through the phrase you are studying, mentally identify the different sounds, dynamics, and articulations you want to give each phrase.
5. Identify how you will make the transition of this phrase to the next.
6. Work out clearly where you will take your breaths.
7. Remember that even if you have a clear idea of the phrase, that idea can change as your performance of the piece matures.

These activities will enrich your way of playing a phrase, and as a result, your performance of a piece will reach a higher, more expressive, and profound level. And your main instrument, your body, will respond naturally to the level of your performance.

It is very important to be clear and precise about the details of a phrase, but it is even more important that those details are based on a palpable expressive need. With this in mind, it is a good idea to place your attention on the centre of your heart when you are clarifying the mental sound map of a phrase in your mind. This will move your brainwaves from beta to alpha. In this way, your level of creativity will be higher, enhancing your artistic approach to the musical phrase, and you will enjoy the process of preparing a piece of music more fully.

Another important technique is the use of slow studying, meaning playing a piece at a very slow speed. When you play slowly, keeping in mind the musical intentions of the real speed of the piece, your brain will enter a space where it can process all the information you need to perform it. At the same time, this creates a harmonious bond between your mind, emotions, and body. Once you master a piece at a much slower speed, you will find that it flows much more smoothly when you play it again at the right speed.

I personally have benefited greatly from studying pieces at a much slower speed. In my teaching career, I have witnessed my students benefit from this excellent learning strategy.

> One must always practice slowly. If you learn something slowly, you forget it slowly. (Itzhak Perlman, 2023)

Be Your Own Conductor

In the development of your mental metacognitive skills and the process of learning a piece of music there is a creative approach that can be extraordinarily helpful: becoming your own orchestra conductor. This can be helpful for various reasons. One is that it allows you to observe the piece from the outside. Another is that it clarifies your musical intentions without your instrument. And finally, and perhaps most importantly, is the emotional impact of conducting your own music.

It is a process that involves the body through conducting with your hands, the mind through clarifying the phrasing, and the heart through feeling the emotions that are to be expressed. To better understand this approach, try the following activities:

1. Choose a piece you are studying.
2. Take some slow, deep breaths.
3. With a detailed mental sound map of your piece, conduct it while contemplating the specific emotions you want to express while playing, holding them in the centre of your heart. Perform this activity twice.
4. Play the piece.
5. Write down your reflections.

In the case of a concert, it is advisable to use the orchestra score and in the case of chamber music such as violin and piano, to have the score for both instruments. This way of approaching a piece of music is extremely enriching. It can be applied to all kinds of musical pieces. It is a way of seeing a piece of music from above, like an eagle that observes the wonders of nature from on high.

Meditation and Music

> Zen is not some kind of excitement, but concentration on our usual everyday routine. (Suzuki, 1987, p.95)

In the digital age in which we live, two phenomena have become very common. One is the great advantage of being able to connect with people, institutions, and events anywhere in the world without having to be physically present there. The other is the phenomenon of distraction in the learning process. Young people today are inundated with images and information on their laptops and cell phones. This inevitably affects their concentration on their academic activities. In response to this phenomenon, mindfulness initiatives have been launched at schools, especially in North America, to help students relax and to improve their concentration.

Both visual motor rehearsal and meditation are used by internationally-renowned musicians, such as the violinist Joshua Bell. In an interview with this violinist in episode sixteen of *Living the Classical Life* (2015), Bell describes how athletes use visualization in their daily routines and how he uses it for difficult passages in pieces he is working on, with great results. When he explains this, the interviewer observes that it seems like a kind of Zen meditation, to which Bell responds that in effect to play the violin you need to enter a deep state of concentration resembling meditation.

This is why making the utmost use of your mental capacities in your daily practice will help you to play a piece of music the way you really want to. The key is to use the strategies described here in a continuous and disciplined manner, as only in this way will they have a real effect on your way of playing and your relationship with music.

Ana María Pérez, the founder of the Healthy Posture Project at Gijón Conservatory in Spain, identifies five reasons why meditation is an important support for learning to play a musical instrument (Pérez, 2016). These reasons are:

1. You become aware of your internal noise.
2. You begin breathing naturally and calmly.
3. You relax (in the sense of using the minimum tension necessary).
4. You suspend judgement.
5. You generate acceptance and compassion.

For these reasons, I recommend taking a few minutes before each practice to meditate. Of course, there are various types of meditation, but a good approach to begin with is open focus meditation. This involves the following steps:

1. Sit in a chair with your back straight and your feet planted firmly on the floor.
2. Inhale for four beats, hold for one beat, and exhale for four beats. Repeat this sequence until you feel that your body is completely relaxed.
3. Keep breathing slowly and deeply throughout the meditation.
4. Place your attention on your feet and on the space around your feet.
5. Place your attention on your legs and on the space around your legs.
6. Place your attention on your hips and on the space around your hips.
7. Place your attention on your back and on the space around your back.
8. Place your attention on your shoulders and on the space around your shoulders.
9. Place your attention on your neck and on the space around your neck.
10. Place your attention on your head and on the space around your head.
11. Place your attention on the space all around your body.
12. End the meditation by placing your attention on the middle of your chest and breathing slowly and deeply from that spot.

One thing that it is very important to highlight regarding the benefits of meditation is that because your brain is in an alpha state, any activity you engage in using the visual motor rehearsal technique will be much more effective and powerful, and thus its effect on your playing will be much stronger and more precise. Thanks to meditation, your brain will become more coherent, and your mental activity will be much clearer and more centred. This is why it is so important to do it before practice.

Personally, I have found that when I meditate and use the visual motor rehearsal technique, I experience my mental sound map with my whole being. It is a mental performance charged with a special energy. This energy will in turn be reflected in your playing on a physical level. When you visualize your mental sound map while in alpha state, your conscious mind will be much more harmoniously connected to your subconscious, and this is precisely where the real changes can take place, effectively and creatively manifesting themselves in your playing.

Something truly important will happen when you use meditation to support your music training in a disciplined way. Your analytical mind, which likes to criticize every aspect of your playing, will quieten and you will feel a very powerful focused energy in which the mind-body connection will be able to convey your musical intentions more effectively.

To experience the impact of meditation on your daily practice, try the following activities:

1. Sit in a chair with your feet planted firmly on the floor, your back straight and your neck in line with your spine.
2. Carry out the Quick Coherence ® technique.
3. Carry out the open focus meditation exercise, beginning with your feet and working your way up to your head.
4. In this alpha state that you have created, make a mental sound map of a piece you are studying.
5. Perform the open focus meditation again, this time beginning with your head and working your way down to your feet.
6. Pick up your instrument and play the piece.
7. Write down your reflections.

By adding meditation to your daily practice routine, the objectives of your practice will be much more focused and effective, and you will be surprised by the wonderful results in your playing and performing on stage, as you will be developing your metacognitive qualities of deep concentration. Allow the infinite power of your mind to create your true artistic self.

2.5. THE EMOTIONAL BRIDGE BETWEEN MUSIC AND THE WORLD OF SOUND

In the chapter on emotional awareness in the first section of this book, I discussed the importance of being aware of the kinds of emotions that you want to express in your playing, how images from nature can be used as a way to evoke those emotions, and the importance of establishing heart coherence when playing your instrument.

I also mentioned the emotional bridge that exists between you and the world of sound. Crossing that bridge is one of the primordial objectives of this new studying method, and if you've been following the steps outlined up to this point, you will be laying the foundations for this to happen. It is by crossing the bridge that you will achieve an authentic, profound connection with the music you are playing. This connection is the basis for a performance that is truly expressive in every sense of the word.

The history of musical creation has been characterized by a number of different eras, such as the Baroque, Classical, Romantic, Impressionist, and Contemporary periods. Despite the stylistic differences between these periods, there is one characteristic that they all share at the deepest level: a relationship with nature. Nature has been the most prized muse of many composers. This is particularly notable in the case of composers like Vivaldi, Beethoven, Mendelssohn, Debussy, and Messiaen, to name a few.

One prominent example is Beethoven's Sixth Symphony, also known as the *Pastoral Symphony*. As its name suggests, for this symphony Beethoven took his inspiration from the countryside. Beethoven was a great nature lover. He often escaped from Vienna to spend time in the country, where he would spend much of his time walking in the forest. In fact, the subtitle of his sixth symphony is *Memory of Country Life*. It is also worth noting that the composer defined the *Pastoral Symphony* as "more an expression of feeling than a painting in sounds." This definition of Beethoven's reminds us once again of the importance of the relationship between art and nature and its power as a creator of specific feelings within us. It is precisely this power that creates the emotional bridge between us and music, and thus establishes a vibrant connection between artist and audience.

The titles of the different movements of Beethoven's symphony all underline this point. The second movement is titled "*Szene am Bach*" ("Scene at the Brook"), the third movement is named "*Lustiges Zussammensein der Landleute*" ("Happy Gathering of Country Folk"), and the fourth is called "*Gewitter Sturm*" ("Thunderstorm"). These titles reveal the intimate relationship the composer had with the natural world and that his mission as an artist was to capture the power of nature in his music.

Another fact that points to how much Beethoven valued nature as a source of his inspiration is his profound admiration for J. W. Goethe (1749-1832), the father of German Romanticism, whom he had the good fortune to meet in July 1812 through the writer Bettina Brentano. Beethoven set some of Goethe's poems to music, and Goethe himself had a profound relationship with the world of nature. Indeed, his relationship with it was so intimate that some said he could predict the weather with surprising accuracy. And Goethe was also a lover of the world of sound. He once described music as "liquid architecture" and suggested that to maintain contact with the beauty of life a person should "hear a little song, read a good poem, and see a fine picture" every day (Readhoot, 2023).

The Composer-Performer Relationship

In previous chapters I have suggested that as musical performers we need to think of ourselves as painters, since we paint sounds in space and reflect before adding the next brush stroke; as actors, since we speak through music and at the same time express ourselves with our bodies; as singers, as we sing through our instruments and we are conscious of the fact that this singing emerges physically from both our breathing and our instrument; and as dancers, because our body expresses the music we play in a truly profound way.

Alongside this new vision of the musician, we could include the idea of seeing ourselves as composers in an exclusively creative sense. As musicians, being co-creators of the music on the page, we compose our own piece, internalizing the composition in such a way that we effectively translate it into something that is uniquely our own.

This suggestion may seem controversial, as traditionally the world of music composition is considered somehow separate from the world of music performance. It is generally believed that composers are the creators, and that the performer's role is merely to play the notes printed on the paper. But this idea limits musicians in their daily practice, as by viewing themselves strictly as players they cannot engage fully with the music being studied. Of course, we need to respect the mission of composers as artists who express ideas in sound, and to respect the content of their works of art. This is obvious. But what I want to point out here is the importance of establishing a co-creative relationship between composer and performer so that as performers we can realize our full creative potential in each music practice. This perspective can also greatly enrich the composer's profound and arduous work, as a strong relationship between composer and performer will enhance the expression of the purest essence of the music itself. In short, while composers record their ideas on paper, performers engrave those written ideas creatively in space through the sounds that emerge from their instruments in response to the composer's creative suggestions.

The main objective of this perspective is to challenge the idea that music is something that exists outside of us. The reality is quite the contrary: music is a beautiful invisible force that resonates within us, and thus every piece of music we play calls upon us to internalize it—to make it part of our inner world so that it can emanate from our bodies, hearts, and minds. For performers, the purpose of printed music is to provide us with the framework necessary for the sound to be embodied within us, to emanate it from the very depths of our being. This is why an artistic connection needs to be created between the world of composition and the world of performance. Later I will explore this relationship between composers and performers further; but first, in the next section, I will discuss how you can become a co-creator of this amazing music captured on paper, like a dormant work of art waiting to be given life. I will also outline some activities you can do to enhance your emotional awareness through images of nature and the development of heart coherence.

The Emotions of the Performer

Before exploring what you need to do to help create the emotional bridge between yourself and the music, take a moment to reflect on your current relationship with the sonic art. To do this, find a peaceful place where you feel comfortable and relaxed. This may be in a quiet room or in an environment where you are surrounded by nature. The important thing is that the place helps you to be as focused and attentive as possible, so that your thoughts can come to you spontaneously.

Once you have found the place, get into a position that allows you to keep your back as straight and relaxed as possible, either sitting or lying down. Then focus your attention on your abdominal breathing, guiding your breathing in order to fully relax and tone your body.

When you are fully relaxed, consider the following questions, allowing your intuition to answer them:

What kind of relationship do I have with music?

Do I feel specific emotions when I play?

What relationship do I have with my emotions?

Is there a connection between my emotional world and the emotive field of the music I play?

What is my goal as an artist?

Do I feel the energy of the music in my heart when I play?

You may decide only to respond to one question at a time; if so, feel free to do this exercise several times. What matters is that you feel completely comfortable when responding to each question, as the objective is to identify your real opinion, free of self-judgement, about your emotional relationship with music and your goals as an artist.

When you finish the exercise, write down your answers, with one column to describe your emotional relationship and another for your goals. This will help you to tease out all your deeper feelings, and also to clarify for yourself your objectives as an artist-creator.

This exercise can be carried out as often as you feel it is necessary. It is an excellent strategy for laying the foundations of the emotional bridge between you and the world of sound, as well as a way of releasing emotional tensions past and present.

To experience emotions that enrich you and your audience, it is important to eliminate any feelings that may be blocking the flow of your true expressive capacities. This is why activities to establish heart coherence, like those described in the first part of this book, are essential to lay the emotional foundations for the full development of our metacognitive capacities of expression.

To achieve a more conscious perception of the emotions that the images of nature can conjure within you, try applying the technique outlined below. This technique can be applied as part of your daily study, as it can be an extremely effective way of developing the connection between your emotions and the world of sound. The steps of this technique are related to the four elements of nature according to Ancient Greek tradition: fire, earth, water, and air.

After relaxing your mind and body with some slow and deep breaths, carry out the following steps:

1. Close your eyes, place your attention on the centre of your heart, and bring to mind an image of fire. For example, you could imagine that you are staring at a bonfire in a forest. Keep breathing deeply and take note of the emotion that arises within you in response to the image you have created in your mind. Play a series of rhythms on a percussion instrument with the image still in your mind. Open your eyes slowly and then write down your reflections on what you felt.
2. Close your eyes, place your attention on the centre of your heart, and bring to mind an image of water. For example, you might imagine the light of the sun reflected on the surface of a lake. Maintaining your state of relaxation, take note of the feeling that the image of water has created within you. Play a series of rhythms on a percussion instrument with the image still in your mind. When you open your eyes, write down a description of your emotional experience.
3. Close your eyes, place your attention on the centre of your heart, and bring to mind an image of earth. For example, you could imagine

walking along a forest trail. With the same relaxed energy, take note of the feeling that arises from you while maintaining that image in your mind. Play a series of rhythms on a percussion instrument with the image still in your mind. Write down in your notebook how you felt during your experience with the image of water in your mind.

4. Close your eyes, place your attention on the centre of your heart, and bring to mind an image of air. For example, you might imagine the sound of the wind at night. While continuing to breathe slowly and deeply, take note of the emotion that the image inspires in you. Play a series of rhythms on a percussion instrument with the image still in your mind. When you open your eyes, write down a description of your experience in your notebook. Allow your thoughts to come to you as spontaneously as possible.

You can do these activities in any order you prefer. You can do all four elements in one sitting, or one at a time, or two at a time. The important thing is to dedicate time and concentration to each step related to each element, visualizing each image as precisely as possible. For example, if for earth you imagine a walk in the forest, think about how your feet feel as they touch the earth, the sounds that fill your ears, and the scents you smell as you walk. All of this will help make the emotion that the image evokes in you as precise and detailed as it can be. In this way, you will be enriching your emotional world, which will contribute to more vibrant and expressive playing.

Being conscious of the characteristics of the relationships between music and the elements of nature can be extremely helpful for musicians, as it not only enriches our emotional connection with music but can also free up places within us that are blocking our natural capacities as artists.

The Power of Conscious Emotions in Your Daily Practice

Now comes the moment to apply everything you have read so far to your work with your instrument. Everything described has helped you create a foundation for the emotional connection between you and the world of sound so that you can use it in your daily practice.

The objectives of the activities described below are:

1. To recognize your positive and negative thoughts.
2. To experience and be aware of your emotions while you play a piece of music.
3. To use images of nature when improvising on your instrument.
4. To visualize images of nature in relation to the pieces you are studying.
5. To develop conscious listening.

6.   To create an emotional connection in your playing.
7.   To foster heart coherence in your musical performances.
8.   To reflect on the changes to your performance after carrying out these activities.

In order to develop a range of internal expressions and to express them consciously through your music, try the following activities, divided into four parts:

Part A:

1.   Choose a piece that you're working on right now. Prepare the space where you are going to study and create.
2.   Play the piece while holding a thought in your mind like "the idea of playing this piece before an audience scares me." When you're finished, write down your observations of how you felt while playing and the result.

Without a clear emotional map for the piece and especially without feeling any specific emotions while playing, the emotions of insecurity and stress will come to the fore and affect how you play. This kind of emotion can create incoherence in your heart. This is why it is essential to create an internal emotional map for the pieces you are going to play.

Part B:

1.   Breathe deeply through the centre of your heart (middle of your chest), inhaling for four beats, holding for two and exhaling for four beats. Do this several times until you feel that your body is fully relaxed and there is a coherent energy in your heart and mind.
2.   Keep breathing through the centre of your heart while holding an elevated emotion in your mind, such as joy or plenitude.
3.   Maintain this emotion while you make a mental sound map of the piece you are studying.

Part C:

1.   Bring to your mind an affirmation like the following: I feel very happy and satisfied while playing this piece.

2. Take some slow, deep breaths through the centre of your heart (middle of the chest) while holding your affirmation in your mind and feeling the positive emotion of that affirmation in relation to your playing.
3. Play the piece from Part A again.
4. Note your reflections about the different feelings you experienced when playing in Part A and Part C.

Part D :

1. Lie down on a yoga mat. Ensure that your neck is in line with your spine, and your shoulders are pulled down away from your ears. While inhaling, stretch your arms over your head, and at the same time extend the tips of your toes. While exhaling, stretch out as much as you can and then return to your starting position. Perform this sequence six times. Finish this activity with the Quick Coherence* technique.
2. Mentally study a passage from a piece you are studying. Hold a clear idea of the sonority, phrasing, dynamics, and musical direction you want to give the passage.
3. Choose an image of nature to represent the passage and keep it in mind while you take some slow, deep breaths through the centre of your heart.
4. Make a mental sound map for the passage, holding the emotion elicited by the image of nature.
5. Imagine yourself playing naturally with the quality of sound and musical direction you want to emanate in your playing, maintaining the emotion you want to express.
6. Play the passage while placing your attention on the centre of your heart and feeling how the specific emotion influences both the sonority and phrasing of the piece and your own body while you play. At the same time, sense the energy you create by consciously expressing your chosen feeling.
7. Before each repetition, define what you want to improve in terms of sound and emotion so that the repetition can be constructive, and ask yourself whether you are really connected to your heart and to the piece you are studying. To improve, try repeating the above steps while using self-corrective statements like the following:

"My playing is expressive and radiant."

"I express wonder through this passage."

"My mind, emotions, and body are in harmony, making my playing vibrant and expressive."

"I immerse myself in the energy of emotion itself."

8. Write down your reflections on your experience with the above activities.
9. Carry out the activities described above with each passage of the piece you are studying.
10. Take a break and do some relaxation exercises like the ones outlined in the chapter on preparing yourself physically for practice.
11. Sit in silence and place your attention on the creative centre of your heart while doing the Quick Coherence® technique.
12. Make a mental sound map and this time visualize yourself playing in the locations of the images of nature you chose for the piece you are studying, i.e., as if you were physically present in those places.
13. Play the whole piece right through, focusing on your heart and holding onto the emotions elicited by the images of nature associated with the piece.
14. Write down your reflections.

Don't forget that you are an actor in sound; to play with truly expressive force, you need to explore the emotional range that you want to transmit throughout the piece. And it is extremely important to sustain this emotional range within you while you are playing, as it will have a powerful impact on your musical performances.

Another very important thing to do to foster emotional awareness is to ask yourself what emotions you are feeling. If they are exhausting emotions, simply observe them and replace them with restorative emotions while breathing through the centre of tour heart.

The stronger your relationship with nature and with your heart is, the more prominent its role will be as a magnetic energy between your inner world and the world of sound. It is precisely this magnetic energy that creates and shapes the musical bridge with the audience and connects you to the music. This bridge will help you rediscover your true mission as an artist of sound.

Studying with these strategies will sharpen your attention and listening skills in music practice and help to develop effective metacognitive capacities. Specifically, with these strategies you will be able to identify problems in your playing more quickly. If you have a clear mental and emotional picture of the structure of the piece you are studying, your ear will know exactly what it wants to hear, and your inner ear will be aware of the energy it wants to experience and convey.

You need to be patient with yourself, as time is needed before the results will become clear. What will be obvious from the start is that you will begin experiencing the world of sound and your relationship with it in a different way, on a mental, emotional, and physical level. This will encourage you to keep up the exercises with enthusiasm and dedication, and you will soon begin to see wonderful results in both yourself and your playing. And most importantly, you will begin to have fun and enjoy your daily practice, which will cease to be an obligation and become instead a joy, with very positive benefits for the artist that lives within you.

The Guiding Principle of the Music

To conclude this chapter, I would like to discuss the importance of establishing a "guiding principle" in the performance of a particular piece of music. This guiding principle requires the creation of a connection between your heart and every note of a piece of music. This is extremely important because what often happens in a musical performance is that the musical intention collapses at various points. In other words, due to a lack of connection between the musician and the music, the energy created during the performance tends to get short-circuited. This can result in the audience losing attention during the performance and the captivating atmosphere that the musician seeks to create dissipates. There are many possible causes of this blockage of the guiding principle. For example, internally, you may not have a clear picture of the piece itself, or you may play it without a clear idea of how to articulate the different passages of the piece in a way that brings together the energy created through your performance. Externally, distractions may arise while you are playing, such as external noises, audience movements, or a physical sensation of a barrier between you and your listeners.

To establish the guiding principle of a piece and thus ensure the full attention of the audience throughout, you need to make use of your ability as an architect of sound. Just as an architect draws up a plan for the construction of a house, you need to "draw" the overall structure of a piece of music in your heart and mind before beginning to work on each passage in detail.

The main objective of establishing a guiding principle is to define the emotions you want to express in the piece and bring these together throughout your performance. Another aim is to be aware of how you want to deal with the transitions between the phrases of the piece you are studying.

To clarify this idea, try the following exercise:

1. Keep a large sheet of paper and a pencil on hand. Draw some lines on the page with the piece you are studying in your mind.
2. While sitting in a chair with your back straight and your feet planted firmly on the floor, make a mental sound map of the whole piece, holding each of the emotions you want to emanate from your heart. Be

as detailed as you can with the phrasing and transitions. Place your attention on the centre of your heart during this activity.

3. Play the piece right through, taking a conscious breath between each section and maintaining the whole range of emotions you wish to elicit with your performance.

4. Write down your reflections on activities one through three.

All of these steps comprise an effective strategy for the creation of the sonic-emotive connection within you, which can be expressed throughout the piece being studied by means of the guiding principle.

In order to create a truly vibrant energy that will eliminate the impact of external distractions, you can use your skills as an actor and enter the stage as a character that embodies your mental images of the piece.

For example, if you want to convey emotions based around the image of the wind, your performance could be made more captivating if you take on the part of the wind itself. This idea, which may seem absurd at first, generally requires some very serious effort to achieve. However, adopting a character in this way will help you to feel the full magnitude of the music within you. This feeling will give you the energy that you will then be able to convey to the audience, thereby transporting them through the art that will flow through you. This question of on-stage performance will be discussed in more detail later on in the book.

It is important to bear in mind that on the path towards a new way of understanding and studying music, you will face moments when old habits seem to come back with more force than ever before. This is a perfectly normal part of any process of internal and external change. Be patient and allow these moments to pass without judging yourself or analyzing them too much. This attitude will help you to reinforce your new study habits more and more every day.

You may also find, when faced with technical challenges along the way, that it is very easy to give in to the tendency to resolve things on a purely external level. Of course, you need to ensure that your physical actions when playing are precise, but don't lose sight of your main objectives: to experience the world of sound in a different way, to feel specific emotions that you can convey to your audience, to resonate with the music, and to allow the sound into your heart, mind, and body. Always remember that the goal is to connect with the essence of the music, leaving aside any apparent limitations and focusing on building the bridge within you to the mysterious world of sound. Try at all times to experience the bond between you, your musical instrument, and the musical piece, thereby forming a single, unbreakable unit.

Acting Awareness while Playing

In this chapter we have explored the importance of emotional development in relation to playing music by establishing a coherent heart and associating images of nature with the music.

One way to strengthen your emotional connection with the world of sound is to adopt the awareness of an actor while working on a piece of music. By this I mean creating a script for the piece you are studying and clearly defining the character you want to embody in that piece. This will develop your expressive and creative skills and help you to hear music in a new and powerful way.

To better understand this idea, try the following exercise:

1. Choose a piece you are studying.
2. Carry out the Quick Coherence® technique.
3. Make a mental sound map of the piece while pondering the range of emotions you want to express.
4. Define the story you want to tell through your performance and your character in that story.
5. For each phrase, define what the character in your story wants to express and the specific emotion in each case.
6. Create a simple script with sentences that describe your story. You can place these lines in the transitions in the piece and recite them (this step is for preparing the piece; it is not necessary to recite the lines in the actual stage performance).
7. Write down your reflections when you're done.

These activities will help you "think like an actor" on stage. This mental and emotional attitude will have a profound and positive impact on your musical performance on the mental, emotional, and physical levels. It will also turn your study time into a creative and transformative process. Remember that you are an actor in sound and a messenger of a musical story.

2.6. SILENCE: ITS MISSION IN THE WORLD OF SOUND

Rests give tension to the space between the notes. (Perlman, 2015)

In our times, we seem to be surrounded by sounds all the time: both pleasant and unpleasant. In our professional and even in our personal lives, we enjoy very few moments of absolute silence. Yet this elusive silence, which is the topic of this chapter, is extremely important in the world of music.

There is a general tendency when studying an instrument to focus on the sound quality that we want to emanate when playing. We are conscious of the kind of sound we want to achieve, and we devote all our attention to this. But do you ever devote this level of attention to the silence or rests within the performance of a piece of music? What is your mental and emotional attitude in the rests when you are not producing musical sounds? What is the real significance of silence within a musical composition?

Perhaps in these moments of silence you are simply counting the beat, as you need to be ready for your next entry; or perhaps you get distracted by things that are external to the performance; or perhaps you start thinking things like, "I wonder where we're going to eat after the concert. I'm hungry!" Obviously, there are different kinds of silence depending on the musical compositions or the situations in which you play your instrument.

What is important here is to reflect on the power of silence in your artistic performance and to think of it in a way that takes you deeper into the music. It is through the power of silence that the most beautiful sonic ideas are born. To better understand this idea, try the following exercise:

1. Choose a section of a piece you are studying that contains a few rests.
2. Observe your mental and emotional attitude during these moments of silence.
3. Take note of whether your attention is on the centre of your heart.
4. Observe your physical posture and your breathing at these moments.
5. Write down your experience of this process.

The objective of this exercise is to make you aware of how you perceive silence and the force that lies in it, a force that can help you to create an even more captivating sound experience. Merely by observing yourself during the rests you are already developing a different attitude towards silence, as you are creating a connection with it that can give your future sound creations the intensity they need.

The Power of Silence

In his book *The Power of Now* (2004), Eckhart Tolle suggests that every sound is born out of pure silence, and that it is for this very reason that we should pay more attention not only to the silence around us, but also to the silence that dwells deep within us.

An exercise that can help you to find this connection with silence is simply to take a few minutes every morning, before beginning your daily activities, to spend in silence with yourself. To do this, it is a good idea to find a peaceful place and to adopt a position in which your back is straight and relaxed. Once you are in this position, focus on taking some gentle, peaceful abdominal breaths. Count four slow beats as you inhale, and another four on exhaling. This will bring your attention into the present moment. At the end of this exercise, open your eyes slowly and observe the space around you.

This will help you not only to start perceiving silence in a different way, but also to get your body used to a state of wellness that you can recall whenever you need it. It is this recollection that will help you to experience silences in music differently.

To begin to apply this to your music practice, try the following exercise:

1. Sit down in a relaxed position with your back straight and your feet on the ground.
2. Take a slow, deep breath with your abdomen, taking note of your own silence, and on exhaling let out a deep, gentle "ahhhh" sound. Repeat this process several times.
3. When you're done, write down your reflections.

Through this exercise you will begin to notice silence in a different way, and you'll also notice that your body relaxes when you let out a sound. In this sense, your breathing is like the physical bridge between silence and sound.

Now, bring this sensation to your musical instrument by doing the following:

1. Take your instrument in your hands and raise it to a playing position.
2. Take a slow, deep breath.
3. On exhaling, play one or more notes that occur to you spontaneously.
4. Repeat steps two and three several times.
5. When you're done, write down a description of what you felt.

The above exercise is intended to help you experience how sound emerges out of total silence. It is as if the invisible force of sound was present in the silence of your mind and in its connection with the source of pure sound.

As mentioned above, there are different types of silences in the world of music. And of course, especially when playing symphonies and chamber pieces, you need to be prepared for your next entry, so your mind is usually occupied with counting the time up to that entry. However, the regular use of the exercises outlined in this chapter can make you physically, emotionally, and mentally present in these musical rests. To make this happen, you need to rely on your best ally on the physical level: your breathing. Breathing deeply and in a relaxed manner from the abdomen will help you recall the sensations produced by the exercises outlined above. You can count the bars while perceiving the inner and outer silence through the proper use of your breath and body posture. All of this will lead to a clear perception of both your own playing and that of the musicians around you.

Silence: Detector of your Emotions and Physical State

Another way that you can make use of silence to influence your playing is by learning to listen to yourself during these breaks between sounds. By this I mean taking advantage of these moments to observe how you are feeling both physically and emotionally in your performance.

To help develop this new perception, try the following exercise:

1. Sit in a chair with your back straight. Your knees should be slightly lower than your waist. Place the palms of your hands on your thighs.
2. Breathe slowly and deeply from your abdomen.
3. Take note of your whole body, from the top of your head down to your feet.
4. If you detect any tension in your body, release it in your mind and focus your breathing on that part of your body to dissolve it.
5. You can use phrases like "I allow my body to relax", "my body is completely relaxed and toned", or "the flexibility of my body is my true physical nature."
6. Once you have completed steps one to five, ask yourself how you feel emotionally. Allow your emotions at this moment to come out spontaneously. Don't repress them; just let them go and observe them. These emotions might include fear, anxiety, tiredness, or frustration; all you have to do here is perceive them and let them go. To release any emotional blockage, take a deep breath in, and on exhaling, let out an "ahhh" sound.
7. Once you have determined your predominant emotion at this moment, bring to your mind an image that will help you transform that emotion, if you feel it necessary. For example, you can imagine an element of nature

that you particularly like and that gives you a feeling of emotional serenity and relaxation.

8. Apply the Quick Coherence® technique.
9. Take note of how your new emotion affects your physical state. Stay a few minutes longer in this state of internal and external relaxation.

One thing that often happens when doing this type of exercise is that your posture becomes straighter, your chest expands naturally, your shoulders drop, and all your weight falls on your feet. Now that you have let go of all your tension, you are letting in an emotion of relaxation and peace. And it is just this emotion that will keep your body in its natural state. You are discovering your emotional and physical centre and the balance you find will enable you to create music in a more powerful way.

This exercise can be used in any situation in your daily life. It is an excellent technique for releasing any physical or emotional tension that arises in your daily routine. The important thing is to recognize blockages immediately and to be able to release them. Your physical, emotional, and mental health will benefit greatly from this attention you will be giving to your whole being.

Try applying this technique to your playing by following these steps:

1. Choose a piece you are studying that contains a few rests.
2. Visualize yourself playing the piece very well. In your visualization, observe how you breathe smoothly from your abdomen, which rises and falls like a balloon, and imagine in your mind both the sounds and the silences in the piece.
3. Take your instrument and start playing. Try to maintain the same abdominal breathing while you play.
4. In each silence, observe your body, and if there is any tension, release it through your breathing. For example, if you see that your shoulders are high, breathe smoothly and let them fall.
5. In the next rest, take note of the emotion you feel at that moment. If it is an emotion that does not support your playing, let it go by inhaling deeply and exhaling with an "ahhh" if you can. As you let it go, bring to your mind an image that gives you a feeling that is appropriate for the next passage you will be playing.
6. In the next rest, place your attention on the energy around your body (divergent attention).
7. During another rest, take note of the energy emanating from the centre of your heart (middle of the chest). You may end this activity with the Quick Coherence® technique.

This whole exercise can be used in your daily practice, at a concert, or in any musical event. Being aware of the power of silence and observing yourself during rests will give your playing another dimension and help you experience the invisible force of the world of sound that lies within you and all around you.

Being present in the moments of silence will bring your brain and heart into coherence whenever you play your instrument. This will have very powerful repercussions on every aspect of your work as a musical artist.

> Every sound is born out of silence, dies back into silence, and during its life span is surrounded by silence. (Tolle, 2004, p. 136)

2.7. SOUNDS, RHYTHMS, IMAGES: MIRROR OF NATURE

> All life forms, without exception, emit sonic vibrations that express their own identity... (Levy, 1986)

Sound

In the first part of this book, I stressed the importance of changing your relationship with sound, seeing it as a vibrational bridge between you and the natural world. By this point you have a clear idea of this new perception of the world of sound, so you are ready to delve deeper into the mysteries of sound and its power over human nature. Later, in the third part of this book, I will explore the power of healing that exists in the world of sound.

Sounds are everywhere. They are both within us and all around us. Every activity we engage in at any time of the day involves a symphony of sounds that manifest themselves in a myriad of ways and resonate within us. Whether it is the wind blowing or the telephone ringing, we are constantly surrounded by sound waves that have an influence on us.

But why do these sound waves resonate within us? Why are certain sounds pleasant to us, while others are not? What is the function of sound for human beings?

The topic of sound is so extensive and fascinating that it would take a whole book just to begin to explore it. So, for the moment, I will merely offer a few short answers to the questions above, in the interest of developing a richer understanding of sound and our relationship with it.

Sound waves resonate within us because we are connected to everything around us. The great minds of ancient times understood that our ideas of our separation from the world around us are false, as in reality we are intimately connected to everything that exists around us, in spite of apparent distances. This is something that is reflected in our times in the scientific field of quantum mechanics, with the concept of entanglement.

This is why we feel vibrations within us in response to certain sounds. What is happening is that at the deepest level we recognize these sounds as part of our identity. In fact, the ancient Greeks considered music to be the soul of the Earth. This perspective constitutes an excellent strategy for breaking down the barriers between composer, composition, and performer, as ultimately the sound that the composer invokes and records on paper is the same as the sound emerging from a musical instrument. These three elements form a whole and complete unity. What unites the composer with the player is the fact that both act as a means for sound to travel so that it can be made manifest on the physical plane. The composer captures sound on paper, while the musician projects the sound captured into space. In a way, both composer and performer experience the same creative process, as both perceive sound at a mental level before expressing it physically, either in notes on a page or through the sounds of a musical instrument.

The sounds come from a dimension without time or space, entering the mind of the composer through the power of inspiration. They are expressed on paper and from there they reach the mind of the performer, who releases them into space.

As we all know, certain sounds are music to our ears and others are not. This is due to the vibration level of the element that produces the sound waves. The vibration level is associated with the fact that certain sound producers emit frequencies that can elicit either positive or negative reactions. For example, birdsong at daybreak will provoke a feeling quite distinct from the sound of a car horn. While the first can incite a sensation of joy that makes you want to keep listening, the second can produce a feeling of anxiety that makes you want to cover your ears immediately.

This is why it is important to recognize the sounds that are good for you, as in this way you can begin to perceive the power of sound as a vibrational force that has a profoundly uplifting effect.

It is precisely this uplifting quality that is one of the primordial functions of sound. If we allow it to, the power of sound can connect us with our most intimate selves, filling us with a peace beyond all description. This peace is essential if you want to express art with all the wonder you have inside you.

If you are fully present in an artistic performance, you will be able to create a true moment of sonic magic. In this way, you can achieve a state in which creating sounds becomes a special ritual, just as it was in ancient times, when music was considered sacred. And perhaps you will find that classical music can act as a means of healing both for you as a performer and for those who listen to you perform.

To internalize this idea, try the following exercise:

1. Find a quiet place where you won't be interrupted.
2. Have a gong, a bell, or another instrument with a similar sound on hand.
3. Relax your body and your mind with some slow, deep, abdominal breaths.
4. Once you are completely relaxed and you feel that your mind is focused, ring the gong (or similar instrument) and imagine the sound entering you. You can picture a column of sound that enters through the top of your head and runs down your body all the way to your feet.

5. Imagine the vibration of sound emitted entering each cell of your being, allowing your mind, body, and emotions to vibrate at the sound frequency of the musical instrument.
6. Keep breathing deeply throughout the exercise.
7. Write your reflections on what you felt during the exercise in your notebook.

You can repeat these steps as often as you like. What is important is that you experience the sound as a vibrant being with the ability to bring your mind, emotions, and body into balance, uniting these three entities into one. This unity is the foundation for playing your instrument free of tensions, a kind of performance in which you and the sound become one and the same. If you truly internalize the sound, it can emanate from you naturally and powerfully. Allow the sound to touch every fibre of your being. Let it guide you in your creative process and on your musical journey.

> And I think that is what I seek in the mind's eye. If you look at the, to quote Carl Sagan, "the billions and billions of stars out there," [*laughs*] and what stirs the imagination of a young child. You look at the sky and you start wondering: where are we? How do we fit into this vast universe? And to Casals saying that within the notes that he plays, he is looking for infinite variety to Isaac Stern saying, the music happens between the notes. (Yo Yo Ma, 2018)

Rhythm

As we have been exploring in this chapter so far, seeing the world of sound through different eyes can open a door to a fuller and more vibrant manifestation of the art of music. But there is another fundamental element that also needs to be perceived in a different way: rhythm.

If you stop to consider the universe around you closely, you will notice that it is governed by a harmonious rhythm. This rhythm can be seen in the change of the seasons or the cycle of day and night resulting from the revolution of the Earth, or in the birds that migrate and return in response to the rhythm of the natural world. Countless examples could be found that reflect how nature has a rhythmic, beating heart, just as we ourselves do. Thus, human beings have not only a sonic relationship with nature, but also a rhythmic one.

Now consider the history of humanity and its relationship with the natural rhythm of life. In ancient times, human beings organized their activities in relation to the rhythm of nature and the cosmos. This is evident in civilizations such as the indigenous cultures of the Americas, the Celts, the ancient Egyptians, and many others, which in their rituals considered the rhythm of nature to be a fundamental element of life. Out of this world view came the "fire dance" in the indigenous cultures of North America, which was and continues to be considered a ritual of purification. These ritual dances are celebrated in accordance.

But in many cultures this perspective on rhythm has been forgotten and our respect for the rhythm of nature is lost; indeed, many contemporary cultures even direct their efforts towards attacking this rhythm. This has resulted in an imbalance not only for the human race but for the whole planet.

The rhythm of human life keeps speeding up. The feeling of time flying so fast that we can barely complete everything we have to do in a day is an almost universal phenomenon in our era. The main result of this increase in the rhythm of human life is that what we generally refer to as stress. It is worth noting that this meaning of the word "stress" is relatively new, as the use of the term to define a human condition only began in the twentieth century. Before this, there was no word in English to define this state of agitation that we all know so well today. This stress causes our hearts to act physiologically in an incoherent way, and that incoherence spreads to our brains as well.

Perhaps after reading the previous paragraph, you're wondering: but what does all this have to do with rhythm in music? What does it have to do with my internal rhythm? A lot! Just as there is a sonic relationship between the artist and nature, there is also a very palpable rhythmic relationship between the world of music and the world of nature. This relationship has always existed in one way or another throughout the history of music. However, the change in the human rhythm has had an influence on our relationship with the world of musical rhythm. This can be seen in the problems with rhythm that exist in music teaching, which are quite noticeable. These problems reflect the accelerated pace of our times and the lack of opportunity we give ourselves to connect with the rhythm of the natural world that surrounds us. You need first to enter into a rhythm in keeping with yourself before you can relate to the rhythm of your musical repertoire.

To explore the ideas outlined above, choose a place in nature and do the following activities:

1. Focus on the action of walking and observe all that surrounds you as you go. In this way, you will feel that as you walk, you are dancing with nature itself.
2. Keep breathing slowly and deeply throughout your walk.
3. When you finish your walk, sit down and take note of the sensation of your experience.
4. Place your hands on the middle of your chest and take some deep breaths from that point.

5. Have a percussion instrument on hand. Allow a rhythm that represents your experience during your walk to emerge spontaneously from within you.

This harmonious walk with nature is an element that you can apply to your musical work, as just as you "dance" to the natural world you can dance within a piece of music. To do this you need to internalize the rhythmic life of a musical piece and make it a part of you, as rhythm gives us a unique expressive force in our art and also helps to sustain the underlying theme of a piece of music.

Once you start to perceive your real rhythm, to make contact with your inner beat and with the pulse of nature, your difficulties with rhythm will begin to disappear and your true rhythmic skills will begin to flourish.

It is important to ask yourself what your relationship is with rhythm, how you see and feel rhythm, and what you think its function is in your playing. Write down your own reflections on this in your notebook. Write a detailed description of your internal rhythm in the world of music. This exercise is a good way of bringing to light any blockages in relation to rhythm, and it is thus the first step in transforming your vision of your true rhythmic nature. It is a way of entering your subconscious and reprogramming your system of beliefs about your metacognitive rhythmic capacities.

Once you have finished writing down your ideas, try the following exercise:

1. Find a quiet place where you won't be interrupted.
2. Sit in a chair with your back straight and your feet planted firmly on the floor.
3. Have a percussion instrument on hand, preferably a drum with a deep sound (these characteristics of the instrument will help you connect with the element of Earth, which will give you a feeling of internal and physical stability).
4. Choose an image of nature and picture it in your mind in as much detail as possible.
5. While holding the image in your mind, play a simple, constant rhythm. During this exercise, focus your attention on the centre of your heart.
6. Carry out the exercise for several minutes while maintaining your abdominal breathing.
7. When you finish the exercise, write down your experience and your perception of the rhythm in relation to your internal pulse.

The purpose of this exercise is to immerse your mind, emotions, and body in the rhythm. If you do it right, you will feel your whole being resonate with each percussive sound, making you feel that you are the rhythm itself. This exercise confirms once again the power of visualization, which can connect your internal beat with the pulse of nature. This connection will allow your true rhythmic nature to rise from the depths of your being.

It is important for you to go back to your reflections on rhythm, since now that you've experienced rhythm in a different way you should take some notes on how you want to experience and shape your internal musical rhythm. To do this, you can use self-corrective phrases that will help you to specify your goals with respect to rhythm. For example, you could write phrases like the following:

-I feel the rhythm in my heart.
-My rhythm is natural and expressive.
-My rhythm is constant and stable.
-I understand and internalize the rhythm of the piece of music [I am studying].
-I dance in the world of sound naturally and proficiently.

It is important to repeat these and any other self-corrective phrases in a focused and constant way both during and outside your music practice. Only in this way can they have a powerful and positive effect on your artistic transformation. It is also essential to hold onto an emotion of confidence when you make these affirmations. This will establish coherence between your brain and your emotions.

It is worth remembering that the rhythm of a piece of music will often seem complicated and hard to make sense of. This confusion can lead to mental stress, which in turn may make you play the rhythm of a piece unevenly or too fast. This phenomenon is quite common in music, and arises, as in the case of other blockages, from a problem that is not merely physical but mental. In other words, if you don't have a clear mental idea of the rhythm of a piece and don't feel it within you, you can become anxious, and this anxiety can create tension in your body. The end result is an unstable and accelerated rhythm. To control the rhythm, we have been taught to use a metronome, which will supposedly eradicate the problem. However, although a metronome is an excellent tool, it is not enough to break down a rhythmic blockage. This is why it is just as important to internalize rhythm as it is to internalize sound, as it is the most effective way of solving any rhythmic problem and bringing the rhythm of a piece into sync with your own internal pulse.

To help you work with the rhythm of the musical piece you are studying in a more holistic and effective way, try the following exercises.

1. Walk to the beat of the music, marking the meter of the piece you are studying. Do this with your back straight, looking straight ahead and feeling the beat throughout your body with each step you take. Imagine the sound of a drum marking the time.
2. Once you have internalized the beat in this way, put your sheet music and stand in front of a chair and take a percussion instrument, preferably a drum with a deep sound. Sit in the chair with your back straight and your feet planted firmly on the floor.
3. Place the stand with the sheet music at eye level and put the percussion instrument in front of you.
4. Take some slow, deep breaths.
5. Play the rhythm of the piece with the percussion instrument. You can do this at a slower pace than the actual pace of the piece if it is a fast piece.
6. Once you've finished, repeat the process, but this time vocalize the rhythm of the piece at the same time. Mark the time with the drum.
7. If you have an apparent problem with the rhythm in the piece, resolve it first at the mental level and then mark the time with the percussion instrument. Remember to use self-corrective sentences to reinforce your intention to perfect your internal musical rhythm.
8. To complete this process, walk around marking the meter of the piece.

Make this kind of rhythmic study part of your daily routine. In this way, you will be reinforcing your internal musical rhythm every day. Studying like this will help you feel the rhythm in a different way, as something more vibrant, creative, and powerful. It can have an extremely positive impact on your playing, as rhythm is a very important element to maintain the underlying theme of a musical work. In this respect, there is a fundamental aspect of the rhythm of a piece of music that you should always keep in mind: silence. It is extremely important to feel the silence of a piece of music. You need to keep the vitality of the piece alive even when you are not creating sounds, as otherwise you may end up short-circuiting the musical energy. Sound breathes in the silences, and if you are not completely present in these moments you will lose their vitality and vibrant energy.

It is important to be conscious of the fact that a work of music is made up of sounds and silences, and that both have a profound meaning and purpose. A technique that can help you develop a better appreciation for silence is meditation, as discussed earlier in this book, as it is a practice that can teach you to perceive silence and to feel the need to experience it fully in your artistic work.

Dynamics

Previous sections of this book have discussed the creation of a new perception of sound and rhythm. This section focuses on the colours and intensities of the sound itself, which in music are known as dynamics.

Dynamics, as the name suggests, give a piece of music its dynamism or vitality. They are generally classified into four main characteristics: *forte*, *piano*, *crescendo*, and *diminuendo*. This of course is common knowledge among musicians, but do we really feel that these dynamics resonate within us? Do we really connect with them? How do we experience them and express them through music?

Dynamics have the ability to create sonic magic—that element of surprise that leaves us wondering where the sound will take us next. This is why it is so important to know how to experience them, so that we can express them fully.

It is an unfortunate reality, however, that in music teaching—especially music teaching for children—dynamics are treated as an additive to the music, as they are generally mentioned but not really internalized. The result is musical pieces played flatly, with no life. In such playing it is easy to see, even at the level of the body, the lack of contact between the player and the world of sound. This is why it is so important to experience dynamics with your whole being, as they are not merely an additive element but a fundamental characteristic that needs to arise from within.

There are two teaching principles that can be adopted to develop your understanding of dynamics. One is through the use of images of nature discussed previously, and the other is the use of your body to capture the natural force of a piece's dynamics.

To be able to apply these strategies in your music practice, try the following exercises:

1. Walk around the room imagining a *forte* sound in your mind.
2. Stop suddenly and stay still for a few seconds, imagining a *piano* sound.
3. Walk around the room re-creating a *crescendo* with your steps (that is, going from small to bigger steps). At the same time, imagine a rhythmic or sonic crescendo in your mind.
4. Walk around the room re-creating a *diminuendo* with your walking (going from large to smaller steps). At the same time, imagine a sonic or rhythmic *diminuendo*. Take a break before continuing.

Now, for the next part of the dynamics exercises, find a percussion instrument that you like. Sit in a chair with your back straight and your feet planted firmly on the floor and complete the following steps:

1. Take three slow and deep breaths and feel how your whole being relaxes with each breath.
2. Imagine an element of nature related to a *forte* sound. For example, you could imagine a storm, a vast sea, or a gale force wind.
3. Play a series of sounds while holding in your mind the image you chose to create a *forte* sound. Take a break when you are finished playing.
4. Now imagine a natural element related to a *piano* sound. For example, you could imagine a gentle breeze, a far-off mist, or the song of a small bird.
5. Play a series of sounds that represent your image. Take a break when you are finished playing.
6. Now bring to your mind an image associated with a *crescendo*. For example, you could imagine a gentle shower gradually transforming into a mighty storm.
7. Play the sounds that represent your *crescendo* image. Take a short break.
8. Finally, imagine an element of nature that represents a *diminuendo*. For example, you could think of a heavy storm that turns gradually into a light drizzle.
9. Play the sounds to represent your image. Take a break when you are finished playing.

The purpose of this exercise is to internalize these dynamics emotionally, mentally, and physically. It is a good idea to do this exercise regularly to enhance your perception of dynamics, which will be effectively reflected in your playing.

The development of a new vision of sound, rhythm, and dynamics will foster a more authentic, enjoyable, and powerful relationship between you and the music you play. Practising will cease to be an obligation and instead become a time of vibrant creation through which you will become a true co-creator with the mysterious world of sound. This will have a positive effect on your playing and on your life in general, as you will be allowing the resonant power of music to transform and elevate your consciousness and your heart.

2.8. THE STAGE

Stage fright in music students is one of the biggest problems that this population group has to deal with in their daily practice. The study of this problem in Spanish education has barely received any attention from researchers. Out of a sample of 479 post-secondary music students at Spanish institutions, around 39% suffer from levels of stage fright higher than the theoretical mean according to the survey designed specifically for evaluating stage fright in musicians. We believe that a pedagogical reflection is needed to implement suitable curriculum plans aimed at reducing these rates of stage fright. (Zarza, Casanova & Orejudo, 2016)

Stage Fright

The stage is a place that provokes all kinds of thoughts and feelings, depending on the person. For many, the stage is the site of an enigmatic force that can energize a performance, making the presentation of our artistic creations to an audience even more captivating and vibrant. But for others, the mere sound of the word "stage" is automatically associated with the phrase "stage fright", a terrible dread of performing in public. When you think this way, you are recreating a future situation in your mind, but for your body it is as if you were experiencing that situation right now. Stage fright is quite common in the music world, and not only in students but in professionals too.

The phenomenon of stage fright raises a number of questions. Why do we feel this anxiety in our stomachs when we think of playing in front of an audience? What is the primordial mission of the stage as a space of artistic creation? Is there a way we can prepare ourselves for a concert, so that we can enjoy sharing our art in public?

In many cases, what keeps us from fully experiencing the wonder of the stage is the fear of being judged when we play in front of an audience. This fear has some very valid justifications, as in the art world there is a strong tendency to judge and criticize the work of others, sometimes without much reflection. The result of this is that we are judged in one way or another and we allow such judgements to affect us artistically and personally. All of this has some severe repercussions, one of which can be stage fright, as merely thinking of playing on stage can provoke thoughts like: "What will they think of my performance? How will people rate my level as an artist?" Or "I hope it all goes well and I don't mess up in that really tricky part!" Before a musical presentation you can be besieged by so many thoughts that really have nothing to do with your true mission as an artist on the stage. And it is natural that if you step onto the stage with these thoughts and with an internal attitude of insecurity, you will become blocked. This blockage can transform your musical presentation into an excruciating event both for you and for the audience.

> Chances are, you know the feeling: the racing heartbeat; the clammy palms; the snakes in your stomach; the terror that ridicule and infamy may be close at hand. (Classical-music.com, 2017)

To overcome stage fright, the first thing you should learn to do is to stop judging yourself, as we are often our own worst critics.

And it is a curious phenomenon that the more we judge ourselves the more we are judged by others, while the less we criticize ourselves the less inclined others will be to criticize us. It is as if our internal attitude has a kind of magnet, attracting positive to positive and negative to negative. What you need to do is to replace the habit of judging yourself with a habit of observing yourself with the aim of improving your playing. For example, instead of getting carried away after a performance by thoughts like: "How could I have messed up that passage after studying it so much?" Or "I didn't feel good playing; I don't want to play in public again," it is much healthier and more constructive thoughts like: "I learned a lot from this performance; now I am aware of what I want to improve."

Frustration can make us lose our objectivity, blow things out of proportion and whip ourselves for them. This has the effect of blocking our artistic development, as it is much harder to improve if we are plagued by negative emotions. Self-observation is healthier and more constructive because you can develop your skills by leaps and bounds when your intention is positive and encouraging and when you know exactly what you want to work on in your playing.

There are two ways of dealing with stage fright. The first is to apply all the strategies proposed in this book to your daily practice, because this will give you not only a better way of studying but also a new and fresh relationship with music, and thus your way of thinking about playing in public will change for the better.

The second is to ponder your mission as an artist. It is up to you to decide whether your mission is to show off your abilities and reaffirm yourself as a musician and as a person, or to act as a channel for expression through which the world of sound can transform you and the audience. The result of all this will be that you will be changing your view of the stage for the better, as you will no longer see it as a place where you are required to prove yourself but as a space where the power of music can be expressed. You will be changing your system of beliefs about the stage in order to play more freely and expressively.

You can turn the stage into a magic place, where you will be able to transform yourself into the character that acts out your artistic presentation. You can become a musical actor and experience the full force and power of the stage. You can take to the stage with captivating energy that will engage the audience in your musical story. This point is very important in this new vision of the stage, as to fully realize the power of the music in a performance, the mental and emotional presence of the members of the audience is essential. Only in this way can the energy of the sound flow in all its fullness through the invisible communication between audience and artist. In this sense, the true purpose of the stage is to transform the musician and the audience in a way that consolidates this palpable, invisible, and power of communication between the world of sound, the artist, and the listeners. It is precisely this communication that "leaves a mark" after an artistic event, which elevates our hearts and minds to a place beyond all definition.

The time has come to think of a classical music concert as a ritual event in which music can fulfil its true mission. It is time to offer truly *coherent concerts* that generate an energy that can foster heart coherence in both artists and audiences. This will bring about real transformations both in the performer and in the listeners. The third part of this book delves in detail into this idea of a format for classical music concerts which, much more than mere entertainment, can offer a space for a sonic transfiguration.

The Power of the Stage

To explain how to see the stage in a different, more enriching way both for performer and audience, I will share with you an experience I had as a member of an audience some years back in Switzerland. It was an experience that had such an impact on me that it is still my strongest reminder of the power that can be created on a stage.

The presentation was a theatre monologue that formed part of the schedule of events for the Pan Theatre Festival in Lugano, Switzerland. The stage had a very simple set, consisting of strips of newspaper spread all around. It began just like any other theatre show; the house lights were brought down and only the stage lights remained on. I was watching with a normal level of attention, but when the actor came onto the stage with a simple umbrella, I was so captivated by the way he came onto the stage that I could feel an energy that drew my whole being into his artistic creation. Even my mind ceased its usual internal monologue and focused entirely on the show. It was as if I had been transported into a dream, a place beyond everyday perception. After the show I felt enriched and amazed by the experience I had as a member of an audience that was present in mind, emotions, and body at an artistic presentation. This was thanks to the power of the actor and the stage itself, a power capable of transforming a simple moment into a moment of absolute magic.

Paulina Derbez

The actor in this performance must surely have done some very profound work to be able to create the impact that he had on the audience. A consciously encompassing creative work can create a true stage presence, and this in turn can have a powerful effect on the communication between the performer and the audience.

Several years after experiencing this as an audience member, I now understand what happened to me at that moment on the neuronal level. The actor came out onto the stage with such power that my brain waves shifted from beta to alpha, silencing my analytical mind and allowing me to experience that moment in a meditative state. As a result, by the end of the performance, I felt happy, complete, and relaxed.

Metacognition and the Stage

There are a number of specific activities you can try to help you perform in a fuller and more authentic way, which constitute a highly effective didactic method not only for eliminating stage fright but also for achieving a new and enriching experience of the stage.

You should start these activities at least two weeks before your concert performance, and do them once a day, preferably first thing in the morning or at night. It is important to do them in a completely quiet place where you won't be interrupted.

The general objectives of these activities are:

1. To raise awareness of your role as a musical and theatrical performer on the stage.
2. To change the paradigm of your understanding of the stage.
3. To apply the visual motor rehearsal technique to a stage performance.
4. To develop a new perception of the stage.
5. To develop a real relationship with your audience.
6. To prepare physically and mentally for a public performance.

Now try the following activities to enhance your performance on stage. To begin, assume a comfortable and relaxed position and take a few slow, deep breaths. The activities are as follows:

1. Carry out the Quick Coherence® technique.
2. Place your attention on each part of your body and the energy around it, beginning with your head and ending with your feet.

3. Feel the primordial energy and emotion you want to convey through your performance. Feel this energy and emotion through your whole being.

4. Visualize the moment right before you step out onto the stage. Hold onto a feeling of freedom and plenitude throughout this visualization.

5. Imagine yourself stepping onto the stage, visualizing every detail. Feel every step you take, slowly, towards the spot where you will perform, and sense the energy of the audience.

6. Visualize yourself reaching the spot where you will begin to play.

7. In that spot, imagine the space to your right, then the space behind you, to your left, and finally, the space in front of you, where the audience is sitting.

8. In this space, sense the infinite power inside you, and the longing to express yourself through your music.

9. Be clear about your intention in this event, about what you want to transform in yourself and in the audience.

10. Now, imagine that you're playing at your full musical and performative potential from the first to the last note of the piece. Keep the energy and emotion of the piece while you imagine this and feel your invisible communication with the audience.

11. Breathe deeply from your abdomen during these visualizations, as this will help your mind to embrace a sensation of wellbeing with your on-stage performance and your brain waves will enter alpha state.

12. When you finish your visualizations, use affirming statements to confirm your mental process in a powerful way. These sentences could include the following:

    a. I enter the stage with a powerful energy.

    b. I enjoy my musical and artistic performance onstage.

    c. I establish a deep connection with the audience.

    d. I play the piece [name of piece] very well in the concert.

    e. I feel great playing the piece [name of piece] in the concert.

    f. I feel the emotions I want to convey in my performance in a very profound way.

    g. I create genuine energy through my performance onstage.

    h. It is also a good idea to repeat these affirmations just before you go to sleep, when your brain is in an alpha state. In this state you can reprogram your subconscious with great results, as it is in the subconscious that changes to our system of beliefs take place.

> I was exhilarated by the new realization that I could change the character of my life by changing my beliefs. I was instantly energized because I realized that there was a science-based path that would take me from my job as a perennial "victim" to my new position as "co-creator" of my destiny. (Prologue, XV, Lipton, 2005)

It is just as important to prepare for a musical event two weeks beforehand as it is on the day itself. To do this, it can be helpful to take baths with relaxing herbs or sea salts. You can generally do this a few days before a concert, as it has a very relaxing and toning effect on your muscles. The use of relaxing body oils such as arnica or lavender can also have a very positive effect on your physical relaxation.

The day before the concert, it is a good idea to take some time to focus on it. This does not mean that you need to study for ten hours that day. By this time, you should be feeling totally ready, and rather than practicing non-stop, try breaking up your review of the pieces with moments of relaxation, visualization, and breathing in order to maintain a meditative attitude on the day before the concert. This attitude will give you a unique power for your performance onstage.

If you find yourself feeling any anxiety while reviewing your pieces, stop playing at that moment and acknowledge the feeling. Then take a deep breath and replace the emotion with one that you want to feel when you're performing onstage. Once you're feeling good, pick up your instrument again and play.

Even while you're busy with other activities during the day, try to breathe deeply from the creative centre of your heart, feeling an emotion of power and joy. It is very important to remember to play the pieces slowly. This will give you the focus you need for a successful performance.

Another very effective strategy is to observe yourself when you feel anxious about an upcoming performance and create an emotion of joy and fulfillment when you think about it. In this way, you will be creating an optimal future for this event because your body will believe at that moment that you have already played in the way you imagined.

Next, perform the following exercises for the moments leading up to your performance:

1. Find a quiet place where you won't be interrupted. This place could be at home, although, if possible, it is preferable to do it at the venue where you will be performing.
2. Place your yoga mat or a blanket on the floor and lie down on it. If necessary, place a small pillow under your head.
3. Consciously relax every part of your body, beginning with your feet and ending with your head. Breathe in for four long beats, hold your breath

for two normal beats, and then exhale in four long beats. On exhaling, imagine yourself releasing all the accumulated tension in your body.

4. Feel the energy around every part of your body, starting with your head and ending with your feet.

5. Slowly move your arms up past your head, stretch your body, and then bring your arms back to your sides, relaxing your body. Use any relaxation methods you are familiar with to release all your tension.

6. Curl up into a fetal position to your right. Use your right hand and then your left to pull yourself up to a standing position, and then bend down, letting your arms and head drop.

7. Straighten up slowly until you are looking straight ahead.

8. Walk forward, feeling the floor on each step you take, and imagining a thread pulling the centre of your head up to the sky.

9. Sit in a chair with your back straight and your feet planted firmly on the floor. Continue with your abdominal breathing and repeat the following (or similar) statements in your mind:

MY ARTISTIC PERFORMANCE IS EXCELLENT NOW.
I CREATE A VIBRANT ENERGY WHEN I STEP ONTO THE STAGE.
THE MUSIC FLOWS THROUGH ME POWERFULLY.
MY PERFORMANCE IS EXPRESSIVE NOW.
I COMMUNICATE WITH THE AUDIENCE AT EVERY MOMENT.

Repeat the statements as often as you want, provided you repeat them with the intention of carrying out what you are saying, which means you should pronounce them slowly (either in your mind or aloud), feeling the meaning of each word.

10. If you have the opportunity, walk all over the stage where you will be performing. This will allow you to feel the whole space. This exercise is often carried out by dancers and actors, and it is very effective as it enables you to experience the stage in its entirety.

11. Three minutes before your performance, have your instrument ready, stand with your feet firmly on the floor, and breathe deeply. Repeat some affirming statements in your mind.

12. Place your attention on the middle of your chest and feel the unlimited energy there.

13. Remember your intention to transform both for yourself and the audience.

14. Step out slowly onto the stage. This will help you to engage the audience with your performance from the very beginning.

15. Before starting to play each piece, stand in silence for ten seconds. This pause is what I call the ten seconds of power. They create a space where the relationship between your mind, emotions, and body will be established.
16. Enjoy your performance to the fullest!

The steps outlined above can be carried out on your own or in a group. They can be applied to all kinds of performances, either by soloists or as part of an ensemble. These exercises are highly effective because they prepare you to take the stage with your true mental, emotional, physical, musical, and performative capacities. They also help you experience the stage in a captivating and powerful way that can transform both you and your audience.

In addition to helping you prepare mentally and physically for a concert, the strategies outlined in this chapter are intended to help you think of the stage in a different way; specifically, to perceive the essence of the stage. This essence can connect you in a powerful way to the world of sound as it emerges from your artistic creation, enters the space around you, and reaches the hearts and minds of the people present.

To achieve this, you need to put the steps for preparing for a musical performance into practice every time you play. If you maintain this discipline in your preparation, the difference will be more and more noticeable every time. This will remind you once again that you play a musical instrument with your mind, emotions, and body, and of the importance of harmony between these three elements both in your daily practice and on the stage.

Think of the stage as a place where your musical and performing capacities can be expressed in such a way as to create an invisible connection with the audience, revealing the true power of the music. Make this your new belief in relation to the wonderful world of creation that is the stage.

The Five Minutes Before a Concert

This chapter has explored some mental techniques to prepare for a concert. As part of this preparation, it is important to highlight the last five minutes before your performance begins.

Usually, a few hours prior you will feel confident about your performance, especially if you have used the visual motor rehearsal technique to support it. But when they tell you that you've got five minutes, your stomach starts to churn, and you may begin to feel a sensation of fear rise up inside you. It is like the feeling of standing on the edge of a cliff.

This happens because of an established belief that you are meant to feel physically nervous right before a concert. This belief can cause a feeling of uncertainty regardless of all your prior preparation.

To be able to create a feeling of power and desire to share your art with your audience, you need to delve into your subconscious mind and change your belief about the five minutes prior to a concert or musical performance.

To do this, try the following exercise:

1. Sit in a chair with your back straight and your feet planted firmly on the floor.
2. Breathe in slowly from the centre of your chest; hold for four beats, and exhale for six beats. Carry out this step several times.
3. Conjure up a feeling of power and self-assurance. Feel how this emotion fills your entire being. Hold your hands over the centre of your chest during this step.
4. Imagine the energy around every part of your body, starting with your head and ending with your feet.
5. See yourself in those five minutes before your performance. Hold a feeling of self-assurance and dynamism.
6. Affirm the following: in the five minutes before a performance, I feel powerful and centred. I truly desire to share my art with the audience.

If you carry out the steps described above on a regular basis, you will change your belief about those five minutes before a performance, turning them into a moment to enter a trance-like space of power that will have an impact on your on-stage performances. Let the stage be a place where your soul expands through infinite sound creation!

The Musician as an Actor in Sound on Stage

Everything described above will help you to experience the stage in all its plenitude. But to achieve a profound transformation of your relationship with the stage, it is essential to experience it through new spaces and interactions with other performance arts.

To develop your performance skills as a musician on the stage, there are two other paths that you need to take. The first is to experience the stage as an acting space, and the second is to engage in activities associated with other artistic disciplines. These two paths have the following objectives:

1. To change your relationship as a performer with your musical instrument.
2. Group improvisation.

3. To develop creative skills as leaders of a group.
4. To experiment as musicians with the disciplines of dance and theatre.

Now try the following activities to achieve a freer and more profound relationship with the stage.

Part A:

1. Find a stage you can use for this exercise.
2. Lie down in the middle of the stage.
3. Take a few slow, deep breaths.
4. Raise your knees, place your feet on the floor, turn over to the right into a fetal position, and push yourself up slowly until you are standing upright.
5. Walk all around the stage. Feel the energy of the space as you walk.
6. Perform a simple choreography while thinking of a piece of music you are working on.
7. Place a chair in the middle of the stage and rest your instrument on the chair.
8. Imagine a character based on the piece you are working on, and step onto the stage as that character. Walk towards your instrument as that character.
9. Take your instrument as if you have just discovered it, and with that emotion of surprise, pick it up and prepare to play.
10. Perform the piece while walking around the stage.
11. Write down your reflections.

Part B:

This part is best performed in a group that you are working with. The activities are as follows:

1. Meet with your group on the stage.
2. Stand together in a circle.
3. Take a few slow, deep breaths.
4. As a group, perform a simple choreography that represents a piece of music you are working on together.
5. Place your instruments in the middle of the stage.
6. Step onto the stage as characters in the piece of music.
7. Take your instruments as if you have just discovered it, and with that emotion of surprise, pick it up and prepare to play.
8. Perform the piece.
9. Write down your reflections.

The activities described above will help musicians to experience the stage in all its plenitude. This perception of the stage will help create a new system of beliefs in relation to your performance on stage, turning you into an actor in sound on the stage. The second path for developing your skills as a musician on the stage is described below.

The Power of an Interdisciplinary Approach to the Arts

For more than twenty years, I have had the opportunity to engage in artistic projects with other art forms, such as theatre, dance, and the visual arts. This work has had a huge influence on me as a musician, as a teacher, and as a person. It has helped me to experience the stage in a more complete and powerful way. In the projects I have worked on, I have performed not just as a musician but as a character in the performance. In other words, I have interacted with the other artists on the stage, forming part of the story. I believe that this has been the most enriching aspect of these artistic collaborations. Simply playing music for other artists is in itself an interdisciplinary experience. But to actually interact as a character in the story is a much more profound and genuine interdisciplinary experience that will have a powerful impact on your ability as a performer.

Every musician should look for opportunities to work with dancers, actors, or visual artists on projects in which they can take part in the stories those projects tell. Such opportunities enable you to experience the whole stage, playing your instrument while personifying a character.

An interdisciplinary experience like this could follow the steps outlined below (the steps described here are specific to working with actors):

1. Choose a piece of music for your interdisciplinary project.
2. Contact an actor with whom you feel an affinity.
3. Work together to develop the script for your project, basing it on the piece of music you have chosen.
4. Define the traits of your character.
5. Define the relationship between the two characters (yours and the actor's).
6. Bear in mind that a piece of music in the context of an artistic collaboration will be different from a piece in the context of a concert, as it allows more freedom in relation to the structure of the piece.
7. Structure the piece of music in keeping with the dramatic script.
8. Define the blocking for the project, i.e., the specific places where each of you will move to on the stage. This of course will be based on the story you have developed for the piece of music.
9. Experience the creative process on a stage—and enjoy it!

10. When you're done, write down your reflections on the impact this experience has had on your approach as a performer on stage.

In a collaborative artistic project like the one described above, take the opportunity as a musician to speak on stage. This will help you to develop your creative skills considerably. Remember that throughout this process you will be on the stage as a character in a musical-dramatic story rather than a musician.

May the magic of this interdisciplinary experience touch your heart and take you to another level of creativity.

The Importance of the Stage in the Study Process

There is one final aspect of the development of a piece of music for performance in public that is essential to the process of preparing for the stage. It is an aspect that will help you with both the development of the piece and your on-stage presence: scheduling study times on a stage during the process of developing the piece you will be presenting.

Usually, we don't get a chance to play a piece on stage until we have fully learned it. That is, after all, the ultimate goal of studying. But what would happen if you could include the stage as part of the learning process? It would almost certainly have a positive effect on your development of the piece you are playing.

This is something I have been able to confirm in my own experience of developing a piece of music that is an iconic work in the repertoire for violin. Having the opportunity to perform a piece on stage while I was still working on it revealed to me the importance of including this element in the study process.

The benefits of this for practising an instrument are:

1. Playing with the acoustics of a stage will give you a clearer and more meaningful idea of the phrasing and intentions of the piece. This will be reflected in your practice at home.
2. Playing a piece on stage will automatically make you more engaged with it mentally, emotionally, and physically.
3. It is an excellent way of motivating yourself to connect more deeply with the piece.
4. It is a way of establishing a healthier and more profound relationship with the stage.
5. It will greatly reduce your fear of making a mistake on stage, as you will come to see the stage as your closest ally in your creative work.
6. You will be developing your on-stage power, which will be reflected in your practice at home and in your performance in public.
7. It is a wonderful support for your mission to become an actor in sound on the stage.

May the power of the stage guide you in your study process in a creative, healthy, and magical way. Remember that you are the character in your musical story, and the stage is your sacred space for expressing your art.

Guided Meditation

Earlier in the book I shared some activities for mentally and emotionally preparing for a stage performance. This final section of this chapter offers a guided meditation that can support those activities. This meditation is best carried out while sitting with your back straight and your feet firmly on the floor, or lying down with a support under your head so that it is in line with your spine.

The guided meditation consists of the following steps:

1. Feel your body.
2. Breathe in and out slowly, releasing all bodily tension.
3. Feel how your body grows heavy and relaxed.
4. Place your attention on your feet and on the energy around them. Feel your calves and knees and the energy around them. Feel your hips and back and the energy around them. Feel your shoulders, arms, and hands, and the energy around them. Feel your head and the energy around it.
5. Feel the energy emanating from every part of your body,
6. Place your hands over the centre of your chest and breathe slowly through your centre of power and creativity. Apply the Quick Coherence® technique.
7. Say to yourself: "I am one with the stage, the music, and the audience. I create magic through my performance. I feel fantastic while playing on stage and sharing the power of music with the audience."
8. Imagine you are backstage waiting to step out to play. While breathing slowly, feel the powerful energy that emanates from your heart.
9. Imagine yourself walking onto the stage. With each step, feel the captivating energy.
10. You reach your point of power on the stage. Imagine looking out over the audience with love and connecting with their hearts.
11. You raise your instrument slowly. You count to ten and begin to play.
12. While visualizing the piece you are playing, say the following words in your head: I feel wonderful while I play. My performance is brilliant and expressive. I can feel the energy of the audience and how the music is moving their hearts. Energy, love, and power are created in this moment of reverence.
13. You have finished playing and your heart feels full and happy. Enjoy this moment. You did it!

14. Count to ten and then take another slow, deep breath before opening your eyes.
15. Give thanks from the bottom of your heart for the opportunity to express yourself freely on stage and to transform your listeners.

This meditation can be very effective if you do it before going to sleep, as in this way you will be programming your subconscious with a wonderful and fulfilling on-stage experience. Remember that you are the creator of your sonic presentations on stage and that your mind holds the key to open up the infinite power of artistic creativity. It is a power with a mission to transform everyone who connects with your sonic art.

2.9. PRINCIPLES OF THE CONSCIOUS MUSICIAN IN MUSIC TEACHING

> We really teach when we say we are teaching to use a musical instrument as a means of expression. (Pozo, 2020)

In previous chapters I have proposed various ideas to make your daily music practice more creative and effective. I have also offered specific steps to prepare physically, emotionally, and mentally for performing in public. All these ideas constitute a new way of understanding, studying, and performing music.

This chapter deals with another essential aspect of learning a musical instrument: the teaching skills of the instructor. This requires teachers to engage in some personal introspection to develop their skills as musical guides, while students need to give the best of themselves as artists and as individuals. The task of introspection will help teachers look at the way they give a music class through new eyes, so that they can transform it from an obligation into a time of real enjoyment. To do this, music teachers are invited to apply all the suggestions offered in this book. Doing this will enrich both their way of teaching and their skills as educators. As teachers, being open to ongoing learning is essential for our professional development, which will in turn benefit the development of our students.

Before exploring how music teachers can enrich their teaching approach, it is worth considering the teacher's mission according to two very different pedagogical traditions: behaviourism and social constructivism.

Behaviourism in Music Education

> For the behaviourist, educating is a technology designed by experts in experimental laboratories: the teacher does nothing more than apply the technology. (Duque, 2012).

A behaviourist teacher has the main objective of imparting knowledge as determined by the school curriculum. The teacher's function is to ensure that the student memorizes the content imparted and becomes an example of satisfactory behaviour. In this case, both teacher and student are controlled by the teaching system. There is no room for creativity, critical thought, or reflection. The teacher uses strategies like positive reinforcement, which encourage students to learn for the simple fact that they will be rewarded.

It is behaviourism that prioritizes the curriculum and requires teachers to ensure that students complete it satisfactorily. Programmed learning, classroom worksheets, and task assessments are all in line with Skinner's behaviourist principles. The student is not required to reflect on the material studied, but merely to memorize the content. Students don't really interact with the content; they are merely information receptacles. This perspective can still be found in many music schools today. This question will be discussed in more detail below.

The following is an example of behaviourism at work in a music class. The student arrives at the class and plays her musical instrument, after which the teacher tells her what she needs to correct and shows her how she should play it. These two components of a class are fine in themselves. The problem is that the student's metacognitive skills in the learning process also need to be taken into account. By telling students directly how to play, what we are doing as teachers is filling them with information without allowing them to reflect on it. As a result, students will practise mechanically without using their own metacognitive and creative abilities. This is an approach to teaching where students take no part in their own learning.

While behaviourism has been the predominant approach to music teaching for many years, it is important to evaluate its role in music education. As teachers, we need to know when to use it, taking into account our pedagogical skills and the optimal development of our students.

Social Constructivism in Music Education

> As it is the student herself who constructs knowledge, learning will always take place regardless and in spite of the teacher (although in some cases what the student will learn is how not to learn). (Zaragoza, 2017)

In the first part of this book, I discussed the basic elements of social constructivism with reference to three of its most prominent authors: Vygotsky, Ausubel, and Bruner.

One of the most important principles of social constructivism is the concept of meaningful learning (Ausubel). This refers to the importance of introducing new knowledge to students by basing it on their existing knowledge. By doing this, teachers can make the new knowledge meaningful to students so that they can apply it more effectively in their daily practice.

Another key concept in social constructivism is discovery learning (Bruner). This involves guiding the student, based on her previous knowledge, to discover the new knowledge we want to introduce to her. This will help students not only to internalize the knowledge but will also enrich their creative skills.

One way to use discovery learning in a music class is to ask the student every time she finishes playing something what was good about her performance and what aspects she would like to improve. At first, if students are not used to this approach, they may not know exactly what they want or how they might improve. But over time, as their metacognitive capacities in relation to her playing develop, they will be able to use them effectively in their daily practice with their instruments so that they can become their own best teachers. Of course, throughout this process, the teacher acts as a guide, providing what Vygotsky refers to as "scaffolding". As a music teacher, you should always remember that you are teaching your students to learn; in other words, you are not teaching them how to play an instrument, but *how to learn how to play a musical instrument.*

As a musical educator, it is important to know what your competencies are and how to use them. You need to see yourself as a guide in the student's learning process and to help her develop her metacognitive capacities.

The Pygmalion Effect in Teaching

The first step for teachers to transform their way of giving lessons is to change their way of understanding a class in order to enrich themselves as teachers, as musicians, and as people. In this respect, your attitude that you enter a class with is of vital importance. If a teacher enters the class thinking "I really don't feel like giving a class today; I hope the time goes by quickly because I've got other things on my mind," the class will obviously not be very productive and neither the student nor the teacher will not get everything out of the moment that they might have otherwise.

Another important aspect of a teacher's attitude prior to a class is the importance of not labelling their students. As teachers we tend to classify students in such a way that constrains their possibilities for development, boxing each one into a mental pigeonhole. For example, students may be labelled mentally by their teachers with thoughts such as "Freddie will never be able to play with any real expression," or "Lila has a lot of technical problems; it is impossible for her to deal with anything technically challenging." This way of thinking creates a kind of destructive energy that the teacher imparts to the student, who will often internalize this energy and feel it every day until the next class. This will end up affecting their daily practice and thus their performance in the class itself. Teachers need to be aware of their way of thinking about their students and their way of communicating during a class, as these will have a huge impact on the student's progress. Sometimes the student we have the lowest expectations of is the one who offers the greatest positive surprises and the one we, as teachers, can learn the most from.

This tendency to label students is what is known as the "Pygmalion effect" (Baños Gil, 2010). This refers to the huge influence that a teacher's expectation has on the student's learning process. If you have positive expectations of a student, this will greatly facilitate that student's growth. On the other hand, negative expectations can have the effect of hindering the student's progress. How you speak to students, the emotional state in which you share knowledge, your body language, and your way of correcting their mistakes are extremely important to their healthy and creative development. It is essential to recognize each student's real capacities and to bring them out through your skills as a teacher and as a human being.

Learning should be a creative, clear, and positive experience for your students and for you, allowing you to experience each class to the fullest so that student and teacher can become co-creators in the wondrous world of music.

Motivation: A Crucial Factor in the Learning Process

As a teacher, becoming aware of the importance of changing our internal attitude towards a class session is the first step towards bringing about a change in your musical methodology. When you sow within yourself a new way of understanding how to teach a musical instrument, you will be planting a seed that will enable you to turn music lessons into moments of true musical creativity with your students. This in turn will create an environment in which both teacher and student will feel excited to make contact with the world of sound and to express it through a musical instrument. Creating such an environment, which is part of every teacher's mission, will awaken the true power of music. Students will then be able to take that power home and work with it every day, making their study a creative moment in which they can make real progress because they will feel driven by the positive energy that the teacher has helped awaken. If your student leaves a lesson with a real motivation to study and improve, you are achieving your mission to be a creative musical guide. This will also give you enormous satisfaction at the end of the lesson with your student, a satisfaction that will enrich you both as a person and as a teacher.

An example of how you can use motivation in your teaching is to talk to your students about the positive aspects of a piece they have just played for you and tell them what they have achieved since the last class. From this starting point you can then lead them to reflect on what they need to improve and how they can do it. When students discover for themselves how they can improve, it is extremely satisfying both for them and for the teacher. Their learning experience will be more meaningful, and they will be able to apply what they have learned to their daily study. The classroom will become a space for healthy and productive collaboration where music will be able to thrive in all its splendor.

A Holistic View of our Students

As I have pointed out earlier in this book, we play a musical instrument not just with our body, but with our mind and emotions as well. If any of these elements is in tension it will affect the others and therefore also affect your performance. For example, if students feel insecure or frustrated, this will block their performance, since no matter how clear they are about what they want to achieve, this feeling will prevent their bodies from effectively responding in accordance with their intentions. This is why it is essential to transform your vision of your students and understand them as a whole being, with mental, emotional, and physical dimensions. In this way, you will be able to help your students develop their metacognitive competencies.

Of course, as teachers we need to be firm and inspire discipline in our students. To do this, we need to learn to be demanding in a wise way and to become a positive guide who inspires confidence, as students often need a clear and firm voice both to draw out the best of their abilities and to develop genuine respect for their teacher. But to achieve this, you need to know how to build a creative and solid sense of discipline in your students through your awareness of them as whole beings. This awareness will help you both to identify how to guide your students to achieve their goals and to give them the specific tools they need to do so. In other words, by considering the role that our students' minds, emotions, and bodies play in their development as musicians, you will be better equipped to help them to solve the challenges that arise on their musical journey, because in this way you will be able to identify exactly where the apparent problems of each student lie and how best to solve them.

Reflecting on How We Teach Music

To transform your work as a teacher and turn it into a true work of art, it is important to engage in some dedicated introspection. In this way, you can take a conscious approach to your mission as a music teacher, recognizing the true value of your teaching.

Sometimes teaching can be an arduous process that requires a lot of patience, both with yourself and with others. However, if you maintain a good level of contact with your own inner being and can find that patience, the results can be extremely satisfying.

To begin the process of introspection and reflection on your teaching practice mentioned above, try the following exercise:

1. Find a quiet place where you won't be interrupted. Sit down with your back straight and your feet planted on the floor.
2. Take a few slow and deep breaths, concentrating on the energy that emanates from your abdomen. Breathe in for four beats, hold your breath for two beats, and then exhale for four beats.
3. Breathe slowly through the centre of your heart.

4. Bring to your mind the picture of one of your classes. Recreate the picture in as much detail as possible, while continuing your slow, abdominal breaths. Observe the words you speak in the class, your attitude, how you correct your student, how you treat him or her, how you feel during the class, and how the student responds to you.

5. Open your eyes slowly, and when you're ready, write down how you see yourself as a teacher, how you see your student, how you feel emotionally and mentally during a class, and what kind of results you get out of your teaching method.

The above exercise allows you to see one of your classes in a different way. It is as if you were observing yourself and your students from the outside, which enables you to experience the class in a much more objective way.

By looking at your teaching method in this way, you open up the possibility of identifying elements of your way of giving a class that you were probably not aware of before. Becoming aware of these elements can help you to clearly identify the points that you wish to improve in your teaching methodology.

One of the things you will inevitably realize when you do the above exercise is that the place where you give classes has an influence on your way of teaching, which may be positive or negative. It will also be clear in your visualizations that your attitude changes depending on the student you are teaching at the time (the Pygmalion effect). And you will also be able to identify the mental and emotional state in which you come to your classes. You will also get a much clearer idea of your student's mental and emotional attitude and his or her physical blockages.

Once you have completed this first step in your introspective process, you will be ready for step two, which consists of the following:

1. Sit down again with your back straight and your feet planted on the floor. Breathe slowly and deeply to relax both your mind and your body.

2. Visualize, in as much detail as possible, the type of teacher you would like to be, and the energy you would like to emanate to your students. Imagine the atmosphere that you want to create in your class and how you want to relate to your students.

3. Evoke in your mind how you want to feel before, during, and after each class. For example, you can see yourself as creative, enthusiastic, and clear in sharing your knowledge with your students. This will create a positive energy that will be revitalizing both for you and for your students. You should also clearly have in your mind the reaction of your students to your new pedagogical creativity.

4. Breathe deeply. Open your eyes slowly. When you're finished, write an exact description of your visualizations in your notebook, using sentences

in the present tense. This will solidify your new vision of yourself as a teacher.

The last two steps above, which can be done as often as you feel necessary, will help you develop a conscious vision of your mission as a teacher. It will also help you recognize how important it is, both for your students and for yourself, create a healthy atmosphere in the classroom, and see each student as a whole being. My own experience as a teacher has taught me how crucial it is to see my students in three dimensions: mind, emotions, and body. This is my framework for working out the best way to help the student. For example, if a student tends to hunch up his shoulders when he plays, it often means that he is suffering from some emotional tension or insecurity. It is therefore not enough merely to say, "lower your shoulders", as this would only resolve the problem superficially and momentarily. The real solution needs to take into account the student's emotional condition that is making him raise his shoulders when he plays. Once this condition has been identified, I can guide the student using specific exercises to relax mentally and emotionally as well as physically. In this way, the student will be able to eliminate the problem completely.

To get a better idea of how you can perceive your students in this way, try the following exercise:

1. During a class, study one of your students to identify their frame of mind. For example, take note of whether their attention is weak or strong, whether their self-esteem is high or low, and especially whether they exhibit any mental blocks that may be inhibiting their progress. Observe how their mental attitude affects their way of playing.
2. In another class, study one of your students to identify their emotional state. Observe whether they seem happy, sad, insecure, self-assured, or frustrated when they play, and how these emotions influence their playing.
3. In the next class, observe the student's physical posture. Identify their physical tensions, as these often reflect mental and emotional tensions. Observe how these physical tensions affect the quality of the playing technique or, conversely, how their posture helps them to play loosely and harmoniously.
4. Write down your observations in a notebook. These observations will give you the full picture you need to find solutions that will effectively help your students to overcome their challenges.

This way of observing your students will provide you with a clearer guide for your method of teaching. If you wish, you can apply the study method proposed in this book, which contains solutions to technical problems from a mental, emotional, and physical point of view. This will in turn guide you to develop the comprehensive view of your students and to identify the best way to help them in their artistic journey in a constructive and effective way, and to truly develop their range of musical resources.

What I am proposing here is one path, like many others, aimed at awakening an interest in new forms of artistic expression, forms that can lead us more deeply into the world of sound and perceive it as something that resonates within us and in all that surrounds us.

Heart Intelligence in Teaching

It is of the utmost importance for teachers to ensure their own heart coherence before starting each class. Your state of mind has a huge impact on your teaching, and it can either help your students to progress harmoniously in their classes—or, conversely, undermine their development. It is therefore essential to check your emotional state before each class. One way to do this is to perform the Quick Coherence® technique, which can help you start your classes in an emotional state of balance and harmony.

Remember the steps of this technique and apply it before each class for just a minute so that you can begin each session with your students in the right frame of mind and the right emotional state. The steps are:

Step 1. Focus your attention on the area of your heart. Breathe a little more slowly and deeply than usual, imagining your breath is flowing in and out of your heart or chest area. Find an easy, comfortable rhythm.

Step 2. As you continue this heart-focused breathing, make a sincere attempt to evoke a regenerative feeling such as appreciation or care for someone or something in your life.

The electromagnetic field of the heart can go to three feet around us. So, imagine then how our emotional state can have an impact in our student's electromagnetic field and define the way we teach them. As teachers, we need to be enriching ourselves constantly, and heart intelligence can be integrated into our music teaching competencies.

Key Teaching Principles

The aim of all of the above is to enrich your teaching. The principles shared below for teaching a musical instrument are based on *The Conscious Musician* teaching method.

To implement these practices effectively in instrumental teaching, it is recommended that teachers apply the principles of *The Conscious Musician* in order to transmit this knowledge effectively to their students.

These principles include:

1. Being aware of your teaching competencies and limitations.
2. Identifying the best moments to use a constructivist psycho-pedagogical approach (learning by discovery and metacognition).
3. Taking a holistic view of your students to be able to guide them effectively and creatively.
4. Developing your students' mental, emotional, and physical metacognitive skills to support their learning process.
5. Teaching students *how* to learn.
6. Generating a coherent heart in yourself before you start a class.
7. Generating a coherent heart in your students before starting class.
8. Recognizing your students' progress and motivating them to improve their performing skills by using appropriate teaching methods.
9. Being empathetic and creative with your students.
10. Looking for the treasure that lies in each student and doing everything possible to make it flourish.
11. Focusing on the development of your students on-stage presence.
12. Teaching your students using heart intelligence.

To put all these principles into practice, try the following activities:

1. Before welcoming your student into the classroom space, sit in a chair with your back straight and your feet firmly planted on the ground. Take some slow, deep, abdominal breaths to relax your mind and body and finish by breathing slowly from your heart.
2. Determine within yourself the intention that you want to pursue in the class; in other words, determine what energy you want to create during the class and what goals you want to achieve in it.
3. Welcome the student in and guide her to perform a series of slow, deep abdominal breaths on a yoga mat.
4. Guide the student to relax each part of her body starting with her feet and ending with her head. Finally, guide her to feel the energy around her whole body (divergent attention to ensure brainwave coherence).
5. Guide the student in slow breathing through the center of her heart, breathing in for four beats, holding for two, and exhaling for four.
6. Instruct the student to stand up and do a few body stretches.
7. Ask the student what her intention is for the class, how she wants to play, and what she wants to learn (metacognition).
8. Invite the student to play the piece she is working on.
9. When she completes the piece, identify the positive aspects of her progress.

10. Ask the student what she liked about her playing and what she wants to improve.

11. Guide the student to discover what and how she can improve in her next execution (learning by discovery).

12. Between the two of you, establish an achievable goal for the piece the student is studying.

13. Help the student to make a sound map of the piece she is studying.

14. Ask the student what emotions she wants to express through the piece and what message she wants to convey.

15. Guide the student to adapt her body posture and movement to her musical ideas and the emotions she seeks to convey.

16. In each stage of the lesson, ensure that the student applies her own metacognitive skills, i.e., try to avoid simply giving her an answer (behaviorism); instead, encourage her to reflect and discover the answer for herself (constructivism).

17. To improve each stage of the lesson, guide the student to visualize the solution in her mind, to feel a specific emotion, and to perform the appropriate physical actions in keeping with her mental sound map and with the emotion chosen.

18. Guide the student to be aware of maintaining a coherent heart while playing in order to connect from this creative center with the piece she is working on.

19. At the end of the class, allow the student to create her own soundscape with a musical improvisation to aid in the development of her creative and musical skills.

20. Be conscious of the pedagogical approach you are using during this process.

21. During class, observe the emotions you express in each instruction you give your student and your body language as you address your student, as these will have an impact on their learning process.

22. Teach with love, creativity, and empathy, encouraging self-motivation in your student.

23. Turn each class into a healthy process of creativity and learning between the student and yourself.

24. Make sure that the student is learning in a healthy and creative space.

25. Encourage the student to seek out interdisciplinary projects.

26. Cultivate an awareness of the stage in your student, keeping in mind all the elements of a stage performance in the process of learning a musical piece.

27. Develop the student's metacognitive abilities so that she becomes her own best teacher at home.

All of the above ideas can be used as complements to your music teaching, with the sole objective of enhancing your teaching approach. Of course, you can also play for the student to demonstrate physical solutions to any challenge they are facing when playing the piece.

Teachers need to act as guides for their students and to do this they should emanate a healthy energy that gives their students a sense of total confidence. On the other hand, students need to be made aware that although their teachers can provide them with tools for learning, it is the students themselves, not the teachers, who must carry them out each day at home. In other words, students have to take responsibility and do all they can with these tools. They also need to be motivated to improve because they want to and not merely to please the teacher. Finally, the healthier and more authentic the teacher-student relationship, the better the results will be.

> Comprehensive pedagogical training of instrumentalists as music teachers is essential to ensure a motivating and motivated future. (Pozo, 2020)

2.10. ROSA'S TRANSFORMATION

In the spring of 2017, I met a violinist named Rosa at a seminar in Campeche, Mexico. I remember very well how the teaching principles of *The Conscious Musician* opened her up to a new world of study and performance. And I also remember her exemplary progress during the seminar. After this event, we kept in touch and in the summer of 2018, she participated in my seminar at the International Music in the Alps Festival in Bad Gastein, Austria.

Prior to the seminar in Austria, we held several sessions to prepare for the festival. In those sessions, we prepared all her material and we also worked on her relationship with her violin because Rosa had past experiences of teachers who had "limited" her as a violinist, feeding her mind with beliefs that did not benefit her musical growth in any way. The process that began at that time had and continues to have wonderful results. The change in her belief system has had a very powerful impact on her way of studying and playing.

As a result of her dedication to transforming her vision of herself as a violinist and her daily study, Rosa participated in the festival's orchestra and choir concert at the Mirabellplatz in Salzburg and in the Student Gala II at the Wiener Saal in Bad Gastein, playing Dvorak's "Letters to my Mother".

All this would have been impossible for Rosa a few years earlier, but by changing her perception of herself as a violinist and by employing the principles of *The Conscious Musician,* her true potential as a musician began to truly emerge and her musicianship continues to flourish, as does her work as a teacher, where she uses everything she has learned with her own students, obtaining excellent results.

> I have a clear and close relationship with my instrument. And this is exactly what the violin means to me: An instrument to express myself through sounds. I have found the way to connect with my inner creativity and to know exactly what I want to hear when I play. I am not worrying any more about my technique because since I know clearly in my mind what do I want from a musical piece I know that my body will respond in a natural way to that clear idea in my mind and that my ear will be my best guide in this process. I simply found my way of practicing and playing, a way that I have enjoyed every second. My relationship with music has become much deeper. When I do visual motor rehearsal, I can visualize the pieces from above and understand how to phrase a musical piece. I visualize the violin to connect with other dimensions, to connect with the source of each musical work. I do not compare myself any more with other violinists. I now believe that my mission as an artist is to show the audience other realities where they can also connect with the source of music and transform themselves

in a musical event. I have become a sonic character on the stage and feel in my heart every emotion I want to express. (Rosa Romero, bachelor's in music education, University of Veracruz)

2.11. THE CONSCIOUS MUSICIAN PROGRAM FOR ADVANCED STUDENTS

> The Conscious Musician Program is exactly the missing component in classical musical curriculums. (Y. Lee, M. Mus, Guildhall School of Music)

The aim of this program is to help advanced students to develop their own skills for resolving their challenges of their daily practice and their preparation for public performances. In other words, the main skills outlined here are the capacity to study consciously with the support of specific techniques and to prepare for performances. In this way, students can turn their practice time into a work of art, and the feeling of obligation to study will be replaced with a sense of real enjoyment.

The program offers solutions to a basic problem: the lack of daily practice strategies, which affects students' relationship with their instrument and their relationship with the stage. It is an organic program in which a harmonious relationship between mind, emotions, and body is fundamental for success. It provides a framework for students to become their own best teachers in their daily study process.

It is thus an approach that not only supports their daily practice but also provides tools that will help them develop a free and expressive interpretation of their musical repertoire.

The Conscious Musician Program[*] proposes a holistic vision of studying, performing, and relating to your instrument and to the world of sound. It highlights the importance of our mind, emotions, and body as a united whole. It is the emotional level that connects the mental and the physical levels. All this work helps students to turn stage fright into enjoyment and a moment of authentic and powerful expression.

Teaching Principles

The general learning principles, which are based on metacognition and discovery learning, of the Conscious Musician methodology are:

1. Objectives and content aimed at developing a healthy and creative relationship in musicians with their musical instrument, with music and with the stage, through metacognitive mental, emotional, and physical processes.
2. The consideration of each musician holistically, i.e., as a unique individual with their own mental, emotional, and physical capacities.

167

3. Attention to the importance of physical fitness as a basis for an effective and solid technique and for the development of the relationship between music and movement.

4. Conscious emotional development and the generation of heart coherence in relation to the pieces the students play through the heart intelligence techniques of the HeartMath Institute.

5. The ability to solve any problem while playing on the mental level through metacognitive strategies.

6. Development of musicians' creative capacity to develop their creative competencies when playing their instrument.

7. A transformation of the musician's relationship with the stage. To this end, the techniques outlined above need to be applied by musicians in a disciplined manner so that they can express their full musical and artistic potential in their performances in public.

8. Interaction with other artistic disciplines to enhance the creativity and stage performance competencies of the students.

General Objectives

The general objectives of the program are outlined below. These are followed by the specific objectives, which are related numerically to the general objectives. The general objectives are:

1. Make students aware of the importance of physical wellbeing as a basis for an effective technique and expressive musicality.

2. Use metacognitive strategies to resolve challenges in practice creatively and effectively.

3. Develop the emotional dimension in relation to the performance of the musical pieces being studied through heart intelligence techniques.

4. Develop the ability to express themselves freely onstage.

5. Develop creativity in their musical/artistic performance.

The program is divided into five modules. Each module is linked numerically to a general objective.

Module 1. (General Objective 1: Make students aware of the importance of physical wellbeing as a basis for an effective technique and expressive musicality)

1. Conscious abdominal breathing.
2. Incorporation of abdominal breathing into their playing.
3. Body consciousness for the development of an effective technique.

4. Differentiation between a tense body and a relaxed body.
5. Physical stretching incorporated into daily study.
6. Development of athletic awareness.
7. Fostering a free physical relationship between musician and instrument.
8. Use of physical movements during playing.
9. Introduction to the concept of heart intelligence of the HeartMath Institute.

Module 2. (General Objective 2: Use metacognitive strategies to resolve challenges in practice creatively and effectively)

1. Transformation on the mental level of students as performers.
2. Incorporation of mental visual rehearsal to resolve technical and expressive issues.
3. Application of a mental sound map in daily practice.
4. Use of the visual motor rehearsal technique for the development of conscious repetition.
5. Incorporation of self-correction into daily practice.
6. Mental self-perception during daily music practice.
7. Application of meditation prior to daily practice.
8. Development of metacognitive awareness.
9. Application of heart intelligence techniques and their impact in the brain.

Module 3. (General Objective 3: Develop the emotional dimension in relation to the performance of the musical pieces being studied)

1. Differentiation between positive and negative thinking.
2. Consciousness of the emotions while playing.
3. Exploration of Beethoven's relationship with nature.
4. Use of images from nature in musical improvisation.
5. Association of images from nature with music pieces being studied.
6. Development of conscious listening.
7. Creation of an emotional bridge in performance.
8. The ability to create emotional awareness through heart intelligence techniques.
9. Reflection on changes in student playing during this module.

Module 4. (General Objective 4: Develop the ability to express themselves freely onstage)

1. Consciousness of students as performers on stage.
2. Paradigm shift in students' view of the stage.
3. Application of visual motor rehearsal technique to a stage performance.

4. Differentiation between using visual motor rehearsal and not using it in preparation for a public performance.
5. Development of a new perception of the stage.
6. Relationship between performers and audience.
7. Physical and mental preparation for a public performance.
8. Development of music performance resilience.
9. Performance of a musical piece in front of other students.

Module 5. (General Objective 5: Develop creativity in their musical/artistic performance)

1. Internalization of music dynamics through the association of music with nature.
2. Solution of musical challenges without instruments.
3. Group improvisation.
4. Development of creative skills as leaders of a group.
5. Experimentation with the disciplines of dance and theatre.
6. Changing the relationship with the stage without instruments.
7. Self-assessment as a tool for student learning.
8. Reflection on skills of self-correction in daily practice.

The Conscious Musician program thus proposes a holistic vision of study, performance, and the student's relationship with her instrument, with the stage, and with the world of sound.

It is time to give advanced students innovative initiatives in the learning process so that they not only find a free and powerful way to communicate through their music but also acquire a new perspective on their mission as artists today.

Proposal for Musical Institutions

As has been demonstrated in this book, there is an urgent need to renew the music teaching curriculum for the benefit of students' learning process.

This topic itself could fill a whole book, but for now I just want to emphasize the importance of teaching new subjects in music education programs, based on the principles of The Conscious Musician. Before outlining them, it is worth highlighting a few basic objectives that music teaching institutions should be aiming for. These include:

1. Create a teaching program based on the needs of the students.
2. Strengthen chamber music programs.
3. Establish spaces for communication between students, teachers, and the school administration.

4. Adapt the curriculum to ensure healthy and creative learning.
5. Promote individualized attention and the treatment of each student as a unique and integral being.
6. Ensure that teachers receive regular ongoing training.

With the above in mind, the following are a few of the subjects that music institutions could consider integrating into the school curriculum for the benefit of the healthy development of their students:

1. Musician and Movement
2. Body therapies such as Yoga or Alexander Technique
3. Theatre
4. Meditation and visual motor rehearsal techniques
5. Emotional Intelligence/Heart Intelligence
6. Stage Presence
7. Interdisciplinary Projects
8. Improvisation

It is also very important to ensure students have a space where they can "recharge" during the school day. This should be a silent space for students to do meditation and relaxation exercises between classes. School demands can create a lot of stress in students, so it is extremely important not only to transform the school curriculum but also to create "recharge spaces" for students to ensure their healthy development.

It is time for institutions to create a model based on the socio-cultural needs of today and to recognize their students as integral beings capable of developing their metacognitive and artistic abilities to the utmost, as well as giving teachers the opportunity to update and enrich their teaching toolkit.

SECTION 3:
REFLECTIONS

3.1. THE INVISIBLE FORCE OF MUSIC: CONNECTING WITH THE HEART'S POWER

> With just a little effort to unlock your heart intelligence, you will begin to experience and exciting new freedom. Your emotional experiences will become substantially more pleasurable, and you will begin to feel textures in the heart that you have never felt before. (Childre & Martin, 2000, p.156)

Behind every sound there lies a mysterious world. We can feel it, we can sense it with our hearts, and we can let it transport us to another time, to another space. However, we cannot see it with our physical eyes. This makes all the other senses sharpen when listening to the world of sound.

One of those senses is touch. We play a musical instrument with our hands, with our whole body, and with our hearts. Once you allow yourself to open up the power and intelligence that lie at the center of your heart, that mysterious, invisible force of music can carry out its mission: to transform your whole being both as a person and as an artist. This will obviously have a very profound impact on your stage performances, which will reach the centre of the listener's heart in such a way that music will become more than a form of entertainment, offering a way for the audience to enter that space of musical power.

When we see artists of the stature of Yo-Yo Ma, Arthur Rubinstein, or Maxim Vengerov, we can perceive an energy that emanates from their whole being. And this is because the centre of their hearts is deeply connected with every sound they make with their musical instruments. By being connected in this way, the electromagnetic force they generate is of such magnitude that they are able to transport the audience to a *non-time*, to a *non-space*. This is one of the missions of classical music, to exalt our deepest and most divine essence.

Now that you are aware of the strength and intelligence of your heart, it is time to open it up to really transform your relationship with yourself, with your musical instrument and with the world of sound.

By being consciously connected to the intelligence of your heart in your daily practice, you will notice how your analytical mind, which can sometimes be an obstacle, is silenced in such a way that your heart and mind become coherent with each other. This coherence will turn the time you spend with your musical instrument into a sonic meditation that creates a space for you to grow musically as an artist. The real solutions to your challenges in each practice will thus emerge more easily, as you will be allowing each sound to guide you towards a musical performance based on a heart-mind-body union.

All of this requires care and patience. You need to learn to listen to the energy of your heart and your emotions and bring them into your musical performances. Such is the strength and intelligence of the heart that it will have a positive impact even at the muscular level when you play your instrument.

For me, becoming aware of my heart centre has had a profound impact on my daily practice. Recently, while focusing on this centre, my right arm loosened up in a way I had never experienced before. I felt in that moment a palpable connection between my mind, emotions, and body while playing. This is when the act of playing a musical instrument becomes pure energy.

Consciously opening your heart during daily study is a process that requires a lot of awareness and a genuine willingness to experience your daily practice from a different perspective than what you are used to. It is a way of generating coherence in your heart, which in turn will generate coherence in your brain, before you pick up your musical instrument.

A tool that can be very useful in the development of this openness is to always ask yourself before playing: Is the centre of my heart open? After asking yourself this question, put all your attention on this centre and take a few slow, deep breaths from the heart until you feel the energy emanating from it. When this happens, you are ready to start your musical performance.

This step can be performed at any time during your music practice. It involves constantly observing yourself emotionally, mentally, and physically, in a clear and precise metacognitive process. By developing this awareness, your daily study will become a sonic meditation that will enable you to sculpt your talents in a powerful and forceful way.

The Quick Coherence® technique can be used to generate a coherent heart. This involves the following steps:

> **Step 1.** Focus your attention on the area of the heart. Imagine your breath is flowing in and out of your heart or chest area, breathing a little more slowly and deeply than usual. Find an easy rhythm that is comfortable.
>
> **Step 2.** As you continue heart-focused breathing, make a sincere attempt to experience a regenerative feeling such as appreciation or care for someone or something in your life.

This simple and powerful technique will help you to open up your heart so that you can work with your musical instrument in a dimension where everything flows in harmony and conscious learning. This will wake you up to the intelligence of your heart to enable you to play in an expressive and powerful way that in turn will touch the heart of the listener. You will see very positive repercussions at the physical level with a more effective and expressive instrumental technique, because by generating a harmonious heart you will be generating a coherent brain. In this way, the body will emit substances such as endorphins and oxytocin, which are natural relaxants secreted by the intelligence of your body when it is in harmony with your heart and mind.

Try applying this technique to our musical performances by carrying out the following activities:

1. Sit comfortably in a chair with your back straight and relaxed. Make sure your shoulders are away from your ears, your chin is lowered slightly towards your sternum, and your feet are planted firmly on the floor.
2. Take several deep abdominal breaths. Inhale for six beats, hold for four beats, and exhale for six beats. Repeat this sequence five times.
3. Breathe through the centre of your heart. Inhale through the centre of your chest for six beats, hold for four, and exhale for another six. You can close this exercise by crossing your hands and placing them on the centre of your chest.
4. Keep your attention on your breath and bring to your mind a passage from a piece you are working on. Perform a detailed visual motor rehearsal of the piece. Carry out this process three times.
5. Take your musical instrument, connect again with your heart, and maintain this connection while you play the passage you are studying.
6. At the end, write down your reflections on how this awareness of your heart's intelligence while playing influenced your performance.

> The heart also continuously influences our perceptions, emotions, and awareness. The existence of communication pathways linking the heart with our higher brain centers helps explain how information from the heart can modify these mental feeling states, as well as performance. (Childre & Martin, 2000, p.30)

The above quotation clearly explains how being connected to the heart can impact your mind and feelings as well as your performances with your instrument. By generating a coherent heart, you will be generating a coherent brain so that solutions to your daily challenges will come more naturally to you and your body will respond organically.

By connecting coherently with the enigmatic force of your heart you will connect to the invisible power of the world of sound. You will express the divine in each sound in its purest and highest form. Daily study will no longer be a time of obligation; instead, it will become a space of ritual, an encounter with the essence of music.

To achieve this connection with each piece you are working on you need to ask yourself at each moment whether your heart is really open enough to allow you to be guided by the sound itself to play the piece with all your potential. There will be days when you have immediate access and others when it will be harder to achieve your goal. The important thing is to maintain that keen desire to establish a new relationship with your musical instrument and the world of sound. One of the signs that you are connected to your heart will be your mental focus during daily practice, as you will be distracted by far fewer thoughts unrelated to your music. Your mind will be in an alpha state of creation, and you will be much more present; you will thus enter a state of absolute concentration and educate your analytical mind to ensure a creative and effective practice. You can then be as faithful as possible to the clear and precise realization of the mental sound map of each work in the studio.

To develop coherent heart consciousness in each daily practice, try out the following activities (divided into two parts):

Part A:

1. Sit comfortably in a chair with your back straight and relaxed. Cross your hands over the centre of your chest, breathe deeply and slowly, and perform the Quick Coherence ® technique.
2. Play the piece you are working on phrase by phrase. Pause between each phrase and ask yourself whether your heart is really open. If so, you will feel a kind of heat energy emanating from it.
3. Write down your reflections.

Part B:

1. Take a slow breath from the centre of your heart. Inhale for six beats, hold for six beats, and exhale for six beats.
2. Carry out the Quick Coherence ® technique.
3. Create a mental sound map of the piece.
4. Play the whole piece while maintaining your attention on the centre of your heart.
5. Write down your reflections.

The aim of these activities is to develop a connection with the music through heart coherence. It is important to maintain that connection as you solve the challenges that arise along the way. This connection will have an impact at the muscular level and your playing will benefit as a result. You will also help put your brain waves into an alpha state, where visual motor rehearsals can have a stronger effect on your playing.

If you learn to listen to our heart, to bring it into a state of coherence, your musical performances will emanate that electromagnetic field, which will have an impact on bringing out the healing power of the music.

The following section explores this very question: the power of music to heal us.

> When you connect to your heart before playing music, you will allow the world of sound to guide you to powerful performances. You will become the sound itself. (Anonymous)

3.2. THE HEALING POWER OF CLASSICAL MUSIC

> It is the special form of music that can move the heart. (J. S. Bach, quoted in Guerri, 2020)

A few months ago, I witnessed the healing power of classical music on a human being. It was an experience that has completely changed my perception of daily instrument practice.

During a group class with my students, I guided them to listen to each of their classmates while crossing their hands over the centre of their hearts. In this way, they were listening to them with a coherent heart. At the end of each performance, I asked the performer about their experience playing. When the last student spoke, I could not help but be amazed by what he had to say.

What he shared with us all at that moment was: "When I was playing, my depression left my body and I felt indescribably happy."

His words left us all speechless. Each one of us was moved by this description of his experience while playing.

Months later, I am still reflecting on that event. Now I realize that the fact that he was the last one to play may have played a role in his response because he was the one student who had the opportunity to listen to all of his classmates with a coherent heart. His openness was such that he was ready to receive the healing power contained in classical music. This experience raised a question for me as a teacher: What would happen if we dedicated every practice to healing a part of ourselves? Would it change the meaning of our daily work with our instrument?

I believe that what would happen is that our perception of music and our role as performers would be much more profound. Moreover, directing our study to heal a part of ourselves (whether physical, emotional, or mental) would give our practice a clear intention, and our analytical mind would engage more positively with the practice because it would be focused on a specific goal.

During my Master's studies at the Escola di Música di Catalunya in Barcelona, I took a course in music therapy. One question I had for the teacher of this course was: If music is therapeutic, why is there so much stress in advanced music students? If music contains the power to heal human beings in various ways, why can we not engage with this aspect of music to expand our perception as instrumentalists and artists and allow it to guide us in a different way in our daily practice?

It may be that what makes the difference is that the specific intention of a music therapy session is to heal a part of the patient. The function of the music in this context is aimed at harmonizing the person receiving treatment. On the other hand, our understanding of the intention of our daily practice is to solve challenges and play better. We are focused on achieving our goals, which is of course perfectly valid. But perhaps we, as players of a musical instrument, could relate our daily practice with the fundamentals of music therapy in order to change the primary intention of our study. This intention could be to heal a part of ourselves or simply to feel happier and fuller after being in contact with the world of sound in a conscious way. By thinking of your daily practice in this way, you could achieve a healthier, deeper, and more creative relationship with your musical art.

The Effect of the World of Sound on your Body

I recently met up with a violinist I had worked with in the past. We talked about our experiences playing music and he shared with me that at one of his concerts in Milan he felt physically drained and ill before he started playing. But by the end of the concert, he felt wonderful. Clearly, by turning his attention to the music, his brain stopped noticing his apparent physical discomfort, as he was entirely focused on his musical performance. His mind probably went into an alpha state, which allowed the vibrational waves of music to penetrate his whole being, effectively curing him of his physical ailment. The music healed him in that instant.

I myself have very recently experienced the surprising healing power of music. Some months ago, I felt a spasm in my back. I then took slow, deep breaths, emitting a low vowel sound on each exhalation. In a matter of moments, my pain disappeared. Vocalizations of this kind puts me in a state of relaxation in which the brain secretes oxytocin and endorphins. The secret was that I did not let my body take over my mind, but instead decided to take the conscious action of relaxing, and my body adapted to this state of mind. At the same time, the vibrations of the vocalizations had a healing effect on my consciousness.

Music offers the gift of healing. Each composer will have a different healing effect. To experience this for yourself, try the following activities using Bach's "Air on the G string":

1. Lie down on a yoga mat. Make sure your shoulders are down, away from your ears, and your chin is angled slightly towards your chest, thus creating a straight line between your neck and your head.
2. Scan your whole body, starting with your toes and ending with the crown of your head.
3. Take a slow breath through the centre of your heart. Inhale for six beats through the centre of your chest, hold for four beats, and exhale for six beats. Carry out this sequence for five times.

4. Now that you are relaxed, listen to the selected piece with your eyes closed and breathing slowly and deeply through your heart at the same time.
5. When the music is over, scan your body again, from head to toe, and take note of any differences.
6. Open your eyes slowly and write down your reflections.

The above activity can be carried out with different composers. It is a wonderful way to perceive music as a means of healing. By listening to it in an alpha (meditative) state, you will open yourself up to a new world, a world that can enrich your daily instrumental practice and your mission as an artist.

If you can consciously open your mind and heart to the power of music as a means to transform you and enhance your abilities as a musician, you will be guided by the sound itself in each phrase of a piece of music, and these sounds will touch your heart and harmonize your mind, emotions, and body, allowing you to experience the music you perform in a whole new way.

> We conclude that music can be designed to enhance the beneficial effects of positive emotional states on immunity, and that this effect may be mediated by the autonomic nervous system. These data raise the tantalizing possibility that music and emotional self-management may have significant health benefits in variety of clinical situations. In which there is immunosuppression and autonomic imbalance. (McCarty, Atkinson, Rein, & Watkins, 1996, p. 167)

The Healing Intention in your Music Practice

The discussion in previous chapters about how to generate heart coherence is intended to help prepare you to perceive and receive music as a source of transformation for yourself as a musician and your listeners. Allowing the world of sound to guide you to establish deeper contact with it will enrich your daily practice and eliminate tensions in your relationship with music and with your musical instrument. This will make room for a real transformation to occur every time you have the privilege of being in contact with the world of sound.

Try out the following activity to help develop this new connection with your instrument in your daily practice:

1. Sit in a chair with your back straight and your feet firmly on the floor.
2. Inhale for four beats, hold for two beats, and exhale for four beats. Carry out this sequence six times.
3. While continuing to breathe slowly and deeply, place your attention on each part of your body and on the energy around it, beginning with your feet and working your way up to your head.

4. Place your attention on the energy around your whole body.
5. Cross your hands over the centre of your chest, inhale for six beats, hold for six, and then exhale for six beats.
6. Create a mental sound map of a piece you are studying, Hold your hands over the centre of your chest during this step.
7. Walk around the space, turning your arms around in circles.
8. Pick up your instrument and send an intention to heal a part of yourself. For example: "When I play, I feel emotionally free."
9. Once you have established your intention, begin playing the piece.
10. Write down your reflections on the effect of this exercise.

You can recall this intention to heal some part of yourself in subsequent practices. It is very important that you have a clear idea of the intention. Over time, you will find that this attribution of an intention to your study will educate your analytical mind in a positive way, placing you in an alpha state during your daily practice.

The idea of music as a form of healing can also have an effect on how we teach music. Teachers can guide students to use the power of music to heal their own physical discomforts. This is something that I try to do in my own teaching. Music can transform your students in a moment if you know how to take them to that space of reconciliation between themselves and the world of sound.

In a recent violin class, I was working with a student on the third movement of Brahms' "Concerto for Violin and Orchestra in D major". At the beginning of the class, I noticed that the student was rather listless. He shared with me what was going on in his life at the time. I proposed that he take the class as an opportunity to feel better emotionally. I got him to perform the Coherent Heart breathing technique and some physical relaxation exercises before he started playing. When we got started, the result was extraordinary. With his attention on the centre of his heart, the student played more freely and expressively than ever, and by the end of the class his expression had been completely transformed and he left the studio with a big smile. Music healed a part of him in that class. He allowed himself to be guided to the emotional state necessary for musical creativity and genuine progress. Clearly, classical music has the power to heal. Each composer will have a different effect on your mind, emotions, and body.

By that summer, Rachmaninoff was back to composing and months later he was at the piano in front of an audience – confidence restored and playing portions of his Piano Concerto No. 2. When he finished the concerto, one year after starting therapy, he dedicated it to Dahl. (Dodhia, 2018)

The great composer Sergei Rachmaninov suffered from depression. With the help of Dr. Dahl, a Russian doctor and hypnotherapist, he healed himself through visualization and music. Rachmaninov's experience offers clear proof of classical music's natural healing power. It is clear that this composer drew on his own work to heal his mental and emotional condition. With the support of visualization, he found such a liberation in his music that he was able to heal himself through it. Because he had this as his intention, the music responded to him accordingly. His "Concerto No. 2" (1901) was dedicated to his doctor, Nikolai Dahl.

You can consciously tap into music's healing powers. Over time you will begin to see significant results both in your daily practice with your instrument and in the responses of your listeners.

3.3. CONCERTS: A SACRED SPACE

> One of the reasons that music can be such a strong vehicle for transformation is its ability to shift our emotions in a positive way. When we can transform our emotions or remove an emotional block, we open the door for healing to occur. (Goldstein, 2016)

Concert music has evolved over the centuries. Since the Middle Ages, the format of how music is shared with an audience has changed completely. For example, in the Classical era, composers and musicians worked strictly for royal or noble patrons. It was not until the beginning of the Romantic era that the concert format as we know it today began to emerge.

Without a doubt, when an artist goes on stage and captivates us with her art, something happens inside us: something important is transformed. But on many occasions, as an audience, we are not present at all. Our mind begins to wander onto issues we are dealing with in our daily lives at that time, and by the end of a musical presentation we may feel much the same as we did at the beginning.

A few months ago, I had an experience that made me reflect on the mission of music today and the importance of introducing a concert format where both the artist and the audience are conscious of the power of music as a means of generating a coherent heart so that they can experience a true transformation. It was a concert at which a number of my students were performing. From where I was sitting, I had a good view of both the performers and the audience. I could feel the passion in the performance of each of the musicians on stage. However, I was shocked when I saw how absent the audience was. Of course, on a certain level, they were enjoying the concert, but it seems likely that they did not experience any kind of transformation, as they weren't fully *listening*. As a result, their emotional state was probably the same before and after the concert.

Since then, I have reflected on the view of concert music as a simple form of entertainment. What would have to happen for us to change our view of it, to understand it as a ritual of sound? One of the ways for this change to happen is surely to give the audience the opportunity to listen to the music in a different way. In the next chapter we will explore a new way of offering your art to the audience more in detail.

3.4. THE MUSICIAN'S MISSION TODAY

> Music is more than just a song on a radio; it is a language that exists inside you, and one that you can tap to alleviate emotional stressors that challenge your spiritual, mental, emotional, and physical health. By using music, sound, and vibration we can bring your four bodies back into balance and create space for deep healing. (Goldstein, 2016)

As players of a musical instrument, we can develop new forms of sound expression and new ways of bringing these to the stage. By generating a coherent heart in yourself when playing and perceiving music as a means of healing and transformation, you will be laying the foundations for turning your concert into a sacred space for a sound ritual, where you enable the audience to listen with a coherent heart so that they can receive the power of music in all its fullness.

To do this, it is important to communicate with the audience in both words and music. Establishing these two channels of communication with the audience will create a bridge between you and your audience. As a member of an audience, I love it when the artist shares something with us. At that moment the musician creates a heart-to-heart connection that helps the audience to engage with the music on a deeper level.

Once this connection is created, you can access the listeners' hearts with our music, thereby creating an audience with a coherent heart. The true mission of music will be achieved, and people will be transformed by this sound event.

To develop new concert formats, it is very important for the audience to *listen* to the music from the centre of their hearts, just as we do in our daily practice. This new type of *coherent concert* involves bringing the audience into a meditative state of listening.

To develop this new concert format, try the following activities in your concerts:

1. Think of yourself as a sound character on stage.
2. Always generate a coherent heart before going on stage.
3. Welcome the audience with thoughtful words of reflection.
4. Explain that your intention is for the music to reach their hearts and ask them to be open in their hearts to receive it.
5. Before each piece, pause for a few seconds of silence before playing. Place your attention on the centre of your chest and feel how the energy emanates from there throughout the space.
6. Imagine your music reaching the hearts of the listening audience.

Of course, every concert has a very different audience, and some will be more open to receive than others. To ensure the success of your *coherent concerts*, keep the following points in mind:

1. Choose your program carefully, selecting a first piece that will be more likely to generate a coherent heart in the audience.
2. To begin with, find opportunities to play with smaller, intimate audiences where it is easier to engage listeners and take your mission as an artist on stage to this level.
3. If you feel that the audience is open, you can propose that at first, they put their focus on the center of their hearts while listening to the music.
4. You can also propose to the audience that they imagine an element of nature while listening to each piece.
5. Sense the energy of the audience during the musical event, and let it guide you throughout your performance.
6. If the situation allows, invite audience members who wish to do so to share their experience at the end.

Something that can help a lot to create a deep connection between the artist, the music, and the audience is to recite a poem before each piece of music included in the program. Poems can create an emotional bridge between the artist and the music that can be conveyed to the audience and help them to engage with the music with coherent hearts. I have used poetry many times in my concerts, and I have found that it gives me a wonderful emotional power prior to each musical performance.

All of these activities will help to establish a deeper and more direct relationship with the audience so that the music can unleash its transformative potential. The aim is to create new spaces of artistic expression that touch the hearts of all participants, which is the true mission of music.

The audience is the beneficiary of all our work as musicians. By taking this into account as an essential part of a stage performance, you will give a whole new meaning to your art. The union of artist, space, and audience will be unique and unbreakable.

All of the above constitutes an invitation to reflect on our mission today as sound artists on stage. Let's explore new forms of expression where our music becomes a moment of ritual.

Like any innovative initiative, this new way of understanding the musician's mission will take time to be fully realized. The important thing is to start creating opportunities for classical music concerts that offer audiences a new experience. This change can begin with your approach to your daily instrumental practice. The more you experience the transformative and healing power of concert music in your own life, the easier it will be for you to create new spaces of musical expression through which audiences are able to experience classical concert music more deeply.

As an artist, you can generate heart coherence and emanate that energy to the audience. However, that heart coherence can only be transmitted to an audience that is open to receiving the power of music.

Scientific studies have found that by generating heart coherence, a group of people can influence another person in their emotional field in a positive way. In one study on achieving collective coherence, Steven M. Morris reports the following results:

> The HRVC [heart rate variability coherence] of the untrained subject was found to be higher in approximately half of all matched comparisons and was highest in cases where all four participants focused on achieving increased HRVC. These results suggest that a coherent energy field can be generated and/or enhanced by the intentions of small groups of participants trained to send coherence-facilitating intentions to a target receiver. This field is made more coherent with greater levels of comfort between group members. The evidence of heart rhythm synchronization across participants supports the possibility of heart-to-heart bio-communications. (Morris, 2010)

It is important not to be afraid to go beyond the conventional. We need to explore new ways of creating sound, to be curious about our own art, to interact in a more authentic way with the audience. The ultimate aim should be for each concert to become a space into which both the artist and the audience can enter with a sense of wonder, just like when we travel to a new place for the first time, and we are in a state of total awe with every step we take. Then the music can resonate in all its splendor in our hearts.

> A musician cannot move others unless he too is moved. He must of necessity feel all of the affects that he hopes to arouse in his audience, for the revealing of his own humour will stimulate a like humour in the listener. (C.P.E. Bach, quoted by Morgenstern. 60, 1956)

3.5 PLAYING AN INSTRUMENT IS SOUND MEDITATION IN ACTION

The impact of meditation on the daily practice of a musical instrument and on musical performances cannot be underestimated. Simply focusing your attention on a specific thing will prevent your brain from wandering onto topics unrelated to your study. Joe Dispenza (2007) offers a clear and concise description of what happens to us when we are completely focused on a certain action:

> When we are concentrating, paying attention, or learning with great intent and complete focus, the frontal lobe prevents our brain from wandering off any chosen path of activity. To keep our mind from being distracted, the frontal lobe disregards signals from the body related to feeling emotions and sensing environment. Just as important, our frontal lobe "lowers the volume" restraining those regions of the brain that handle sensory as well as motor information. It also quiets down the motor cortex so that when we are paying attention or focusing, we tend to get very still. That is because the motor functions to that part of the brain get slowed down or turned off; we actually move into a state of trance, and the body follows. (Dispenza, 2007)

To achieve the state described by Dispenza, you need to train your mind to reach that "state of trance", which can be of great help to play any musical instrument. How often have you been playing your instrument when you realize that your mind has been wandering onto other things that are not related to your practice? This is where meditation can play a fundamental role by helping you to train your mind to keep focused in your daily study.

The "Meditation and Music" section of this book discusses open-focus meditation and the benefits of open-mindedness. To delve a little further into this idea, try the following activities, divided into two parts:

Part A:

1.   Sit in a chair with your back straight and your feet firmly planted on the floor. Make sure your back is straight. Lower your chin slightly towards your sternum to create a straight line from your spine to your neck.
2.   Inhale through your abdomen for six beats, hold for four, and exhale for another six. With each exhalation, release any tension built up in your body.
3.   Complete an open-focus meditation (divergent attention), placing your attention on the energy around each part of your body, starting with your feet and ending with your head.

4. Place your attention on the energy around your whole body. Breathe slowly.

5. At the end, cross your hands over the centre of your chest and breathe slowly from that centre.

Part B:

1. Choose a piece of music from your repertoire.
2. Get in position to play.
3. Breathe slowly through the centre of your chest.
4. Complete the open-focus meditation (divergent attention) without playing. Repeat it starting with your head and ending with your feet.
5. Start playing your instrument, while keeping your attention on the energy around your body.
6. Write down your reflections.

With these activities, over time you will develop the metacognitive ability to play your musical instrument as a sound meditation. This takes time and patience, but the results can be amazing, as you will be using your true mental capacities in an effective and powerful way. You may find at first that your body wants to distract you during open-focus meditation. In such moments, simply observe the distraction and bring your mind back to the present moment.

In September 2019, I had the great fortune to conduct a week-long seminar with Joe Dispenza, where he offered talks on the neuroscience behind meditation, and we carried out several meditations during the day. This event was a life-changing experience because one of its main objectives was to adapt the body to a new way of thinking: to a new mind. One of the challenges at the event was to complete a six-hour meditation. Participants were permitted the option of two short breaks during the mediation, but I decided to stay the whole time. In the second part of the meditation, my body was constantly making itself felt, and I began thinking: "Because I'm staying, my body is starting to hurt; I'll have to leave." I then realized that my body was turning into my mind! So, I constantly brought my mind back into the present moment. The third part of the meditation was a moment of revelation for me: My body no longer bothered me, and I felt an extraordinary sensation of peace and happiness. I knew at that moment that I had succeeded in conditioning my body to a new mind. Since then, I have meditated every day and have enjoyed great results not only on a personal level but also in my work with my musical instrument and in my music teaching. Meditation can help you tap into the amazing mental potential that lies deep within you, so that you can offer musical performances that will transform both you and your listening audience.

3.6. ROGERIO'S TRANSFORMATION: A COHERENT HEART IN THE MUSIC PERFORMER

> Within each of us lies an immense power of creation. Within each of us lies a beating heart that desires to connect with our musical art. Within each of us lies a body language capable of transmitting the sonic messages of our infinite minds in a sublime way. (Anonymous)

The first time I heard Rogerio play was in 2017 at a course in Campeche, Mexico. His exceptional talent and potential were evident at once, and over the course of a few days, he demonstrated a remarkable transformation in his interpretation of Cesar Franck's "Sonata" by applying the didactic of *The Conscious Musician*. When discussing his wonderful performance in the final presentation, he remarked: "For the first time performing onstage, I didn't feel like I was stepping into the Colosseum to face the lions." This marked the beginning of a profound transformation in his relationship with the violin and with music.

In 2019, I had the opportunity of working with Rogerio again, at a seminar I taught in Toronto. This time, we worked on the first movement of Brahms' "Concerto in D Major for Violin and Orchestra". For Rogerio, this experience represented not only the continuation of the work we had begun together in 2017, but also his debut as a violinist on the international stage. In this seminar, we worked on the principles of *The Conscious Musician*, along with movement and yoga workshops. This seminar was also the first time I began applying meditation as part of the study process.

Rogerio's transformation through the Conscious Musician Program unfolded as follows:

1. Through mental sound mapping, he was able to clarify in his mind the phrasings and precise musical intentions he wanted for the piece he was studying.
2. By evoking images of nature related to the piece, he was able to develop a conscious emotional connection with his musical performance.
3. By carrying out physical exercises prior to each practice and participating in the yoga workshop, he came to understand the need to see his physical state as the basis for a free and expressive musical technique.
4. Thanks to the music and movement workshop, his expression and phrasing in Vivaldi's "Double Concerto in A Minor" and in Brahms' "D Major Concerto" was clear and forceful.

5. By developing his metacognitive abilities for practice, he became his own best teacher at home.

6. He experienced meditation for the first time and its effects on its playing were remarkable. He developed an extraordinary capacity for concentration by passing his brain waves from beta to alpha through meditation. This positively reinforced his mental, emotional, and physical connection to the Brahms Concerto.

7. While performing in the final presentation of the seminar he became an actor in sound, connecting with the spectators and touching their hearts on the day.

The communication we achieved throughout this process was highly collaborative and creative. We both grew from the process of learning and teaching violin and music.

Rogerio was taken to a deeper level of musical performance not only by the disciplined application of the principles of the Conscious Musician but also by the development of his metacognitive competence in establishing a harmonious heart before playing and during his study process. By applying Coherent Heart breathing, he also achieved a deeper connection with the pieces he was studying. When you use this type of breathing, your heart becomes coherent and sends these signals to the brain, thereby connecting it to the intelligence of your heart. It is from this space that his artistic development took such an important leap.

This breathing technique was applied in Rogerio's study process in the following way:

1. Before starting the class he would perform a body relaxation exercise.

2. At the end of this relaxation, I would guide him to place all his attention on the centre of his heart.

3. I would instruct him to take slow, deep breaths through the creative centre of his heart, applying the Quick Coherence® technique.

4. Once a state of harmony between his heart and mind had been achieved, we would begin the collaborative work of the class.

5. During the class, we would make sure that he was connected through his heart to the piece he was working on by means of the simple question: "Is my heart open and connected to this musical phrase?"

Rogerio's conscious connection with the intelligence of his heart in relation to his study process had the following benefits:

1. It allowed the sound to guide him to phrase clearly and expressively.

2. It produced subtle yet forceful changes to the quality of his sound.

3. He developed an authentic and powerful stage presence.
4. He was able to create in a harmonious and focused space.
5. He established a deep connection to every aspect of the piece of music he was studying.
6. He felt fulfilled when playing the violin.
7. He was able to solve challenges that arose in practice in creative ways.
8. He became conscious as an artist of his ability to transform the heart of the listener.

As a result of this whole process, Rogerio offered a highly successful performance of Antonio Vivaldi's "Winter" and Piazzolla's "Seasons" as a soloist with a Mexican orchestra in one of the most beautiful theatres in Mexico. It was the power of his heart and his extraordinary talent that achieved all this, realizing his passion and motivation to grow as a human being and an artist convinced of the mission of his art today: to be a channel for expressing sound that can transform the heart of the listener.

> Inside our hearts lies the pathway to our greatest talents. Listen to your voice so that the power of your spirit can manifest every time you play your instrument. (Anonymous)

Conclusion

The purpose of this book has been to propose a new way of approaching and experiencing music. The techniques described here aim to create a new connection between our essence and the essence of the world of sound. They comprise a path that can lead us, if we so desire, to discover the powerful influence of music in the human being and the privilege of being in contact with music every day.

This book is intended merely as a guide whose aim is to open your senses to new ways of studying and playing music, which will enhance your already rich artistic journey. My hope has been simply to stimulate the search for a deeper relationship with the world of sound and with your musical instrument. This requires a great deal of internal and external work, but the fruits of that labour are incredible if you approach it with fervour, love, and dedication. There may be moments of doubt that will lead you to fall back on old habits; this is completely normal. The important thing is to recognize when this happens, not to give up, and to forge ahead. This persistence will result in very satisfying results that will appear in due time.

Remember that all of us have been given great gifts. It is up to us to channel those gifts in a healthy and constructive way so that they can blossom naturally. This blossoming is what music seeks in us. The more perceptive you are to this message, the stronger its impact will be on you and on all that surrounds you.

Open your mind and your heart to the world of sound. Let yourself be moved by its magic. Deepen and renew your relationship with your art every day. Discover new things every moment. Climb the mountain with energy, courage, and conviction. Reach the first summit with a feeling of triumph and let that feeling push you on to the next summit. Keep your eyes forward. Nothing will block your path if you don't let it. Listen always to your intuition and pay attention to your voice, as it is what will lead you to achieve your greatest goals. May the power of music beat always in your heart.

Appendix A: Summary of tips

Trust in the creative process.

Give everything of yourself in each practice.

Pursue as much as possible a constant connection between mind, emotions, and body in your work as an artist.

Listen as much as possible to the signs sent by your body, as they are a reflection of your mind and emotions.

Breathe consciously from your abdomen.

Meditate a few minutes every day if possible.

Have a clear mental plan for the pieces you are studying.

Feel the emotions that you want to emanate consciously in your playing.

Focus on the solutions, not on the problems.

Don't repeat a passage without reflecting on why.

Whenever a negative thought about you or your playing arises, acknowledge it, and let it go or replace it with a constructive thought.

Whenever confusion begins to arise in your practice, take a break, relax with some deep breaths, and review your mental study plan.

Never study when you're angry, tired, sluggish, or feeling obligated, because these emotions will undermine any possibility of progress in your practice.

Try to start every practice session with a good attitude.

Always prepare yourself physically before each practice.

As much as possible, do exercises that will develop your relationship and direct engagement with sound.

Observe nature and allow its power to nourish your playing.

Create a connection with the listener.

Always listen to your intuition.

Turn your practice sessions into a process filled with creativity, enjoyment, and true progress.

Renew yourself constantly.

Be open to new ideas, directions, and forms of artistic creation that can enhance your musical development.

Never stop seeking.

Experience different forms of musical expression that you feel can enrich your work as a musician.

Foster a genuine connection between yourself, the music, the composer, and your instrument, and whenever you sense a gap opening up between them, reflect on why and seek out a way to reconnect them.

Keep a clear sense of your goals as an artist and a person, as in this way things will fall into place so that you can meet your goals successfully and effectively at the right moment.

Let the sound and rhythm guide you to express them in full splendour.

Develop your metacognitive competencies in each practice as they will help you to become your own best teacher.

Always listen to your heart.

Quick Coherence Technique

The Quick Coherence® technique to establish a coherent heart, as recommended by the HeartMath Institute (HeartMath is a registered trademark of Quantum Intech, Inc. For all HeartMath trademarks go to www.heartmath.com/trademarks):

> **Step 1.** Focus your attention on the area of the heart. Imagine your breath is flowing in and out of your heart or chest area, breathing a little slower and deeper than usual. Find an easy rhythm that is comfortable.
>
> **Step 2.** As you continue heart-focused breathing, make a sincere attempt to experience a regenerative feeling such as appreciation or care for someone or something in your life.

Appendix B: Examples of self-correction phrases

Tuning

I am free of tensions.
My tuning is perfect.
I am brilliantly and perfectly in key.
My fingers fall perfectly into place.
I hear the exact key in my mind and my fingers respond to this naturally.
I play the exact notes I am aiming to play.

Changes of position

I am free of tensions.
I make position changes swiftly and precisely.
My arms and fingers respond naturally and effectively.
I make position changes decisively.
I know the exact place for my fingers on each change of position.
I allow my fingers to find the perfect place.

Coordination

I am free of tensions.
My coordination is natural and precise.
I coordinate the movements of my arms and hands perfectly.
I have perfect coordination.
My coordination is harmonious and effective.
My whole body is perfectly coordinated when I play.
I move my arms and elbows in harmony with the music.
My abdominal breathing is always in time with the music.

Articulation

I am free of tensions.
My *staccato* is precise.
I join one sound to the next as if they were a single sound.
My *vibrato* is ample, expressive, and free.
My *vibrato* reflects the expression I want to convey.
I find the right place to play a precise *spiccato*.
I have a clear picture in my mind of an excellent technique.
My body responds naturally to my technical goals.

Posture

I am free of tensions.

My shoulders are always down and relaxed when I play.

I let all my weight fall on my feet.

I feel physically relaxed and toned.

My body has the energy I need to play.

My legs, waist, back, and neck are in perfect alignment.

My neck is loose and flexible.

I keep my back straight when I play.

I breathe from my abdomen continually when I play.

I feel physically comfortable when I play my musical instrument.

My bodily expression is in harmony with my musical expression.

My body feels free of tensions before, during and after each practice.

Sound quality

I emanate an expressive and profound level of sound.

My sound level is vibrant.

I allow the true sound to flow through my playing.

I am in contact with the sound through my breathing.

I create sounds that reflect the emotions I want to convey.

My sound is an authentic reflection of my images of nature.

I create an ample and penetrating sound that touches the hearts of my audience.

I allow myself to be in inner silence so that the sound can emerge with all its force.

My body responds naturally to the sounds that I want to emanate.

Expressiveness

I am expressive.

I express myself through music.

I feel each emotion that I want to convey clearly inside me.

I find a perfect image that matches the emotion I want to emanate.

I allow the music to touch me and provoke specific emotions in me.

I have a clear picture in my mind of the range of emotions that I want to convey through my playing.

I create a vibrant energy in myself, in the audience, and in the space where I play.

I express specific emotions through music.

I express joy, strength, melancholy, and passion.

I create from the center of my heart.

Through my playing I inspire these emotions in my audience.

Musical phrasing

My phrasing is clear, natural, and convincing.

I internalize each phrase.

I have a clear picture in my mind of the musical direction of each phrase.

I breathe continually from my abdomen.

I connect all the phrases of a piece as if it were a single phrase.

I allow the phrasing itself to guide me.

I am present in the moments of silence.

I convey the underlying theme in the piece of music I am playing.

Rhythm and dynamics

I have a natural, stable rhythm.

My rhythm is clear and expressive.

I play with the musical times, maintaining the natural rhythm of the music.

I feel the rhythm throughout my body.

The rhythm forms part of me and I express it naturally.

I internalize the rhythm of the music.

My dynamics are clear and expressive.

I find the right element of nature for each musical dynamic.

The dynamics are expressed naturally through the actions of my body.

I have a clear idea of the dynamics I want to convey.

I mold sounds vibrantly and expressively through the dynamics.

The dynamics form part of my inner being.

The above affirmations can be used before or after correcting a problem at the mental level. After some practice they can even be used at the same time, i.e., while visualizing the correction mentally you can use the affirmation that goes with it. This will depend on the process of each individual.

These affirmations can also be used according to the needs that arise in your music practice. An important feature of these affirmations is that they reflect the fact that we need to stop focusing on our apparent problems and focus instead on the solutions. This is one of the radical changes needed in your mental attitude as part of this method. In short, thinking about the solutions rather than the problems will help you resolve the issues more quickly and effectively. It is also important to highlight that while these self-affirmations are an excellent support device, they cannot substitute the hard work of music practice. They are simply a way of reinforcing that work.

It is very important when using these self-corrections to place your attention on the centre of your heart and maintain an elevated emotion, such as plenitude and joy. In this way, you will shift your brainwaves from beta to alpha so that your conscious mind will be in harmony with your subconscious. This in turn will ensure that your intentions are effectively and powerfully realized.

As noted previously in this book, all these techniques take time and work to be fully integrated into your daily practice. The results will depend on your dedication and perseverance in each practice session. What matters most is that you internalize the genuine intention to establish a new relationship with your musical instrument and with the world of sound. This intention is what will help you recognize your true abilities and to apply them to your mission as a musician.

On the question of the power of the mind, consider the following passage from the classic Taoist text, the *Hui Ming King*:

"A radiance of Light surrounds the world of the mind.
We forget each other, quiet and pure, all-powerful and empty.
Emptiness is lighted up by the radiance of the Heart of Heaven.
The sea is smooth and mirrors the moon on its surface.
The clouds vanish in blue space.
The mountains shine clear.
Consciousness dissolves itself in vision.
The disk of the moon floats solitary."

Hui Ming King, quoted by Jung, p.69

In the book *The Secret of the Golden Flower*, Carl Jung offers a clear and profound interpretation of this passage. "The pupil," Jung tells us, "Is taught how he must concentrate on the Light of the inmost region, and, at the same time, free himself from all outer and inner bondage. [...] Therefore, consciousness is no longer preoccupied with compulsive motives, but becomes vision, as the Chinese text very aptly says."

Jung's reflection on this passage is very thought-provoking. It could be said that its reference to the consciousness that "dissolves itself in vision" is an excellent definition of how our minds, when free of prejudices and fears, are capable of simply looking on and uniting with existence itself, which is the source of the radiance of the Light. It is precisely in this state of consciousness that music can be expressed in all its magnificent splendour. In this way, our minds will fuse with the sonic consciousness, thereby creating a unity in which art finds its true home.

Bibliography

Baños,G. (2010). *El Efecto Pigmalión en el Aula*. Innovación y Experiencias Educativas, revista digital.

Brennan, R. (1992). *La Técnica Alexander*. Milan: Grupo Editoriale Armenia.

Brulé, D. (2018). *Just Breathe*. New York: Enliven Atria Books.

Bravo, E. (2019). *15 titanes de música clásica con vidas tan turbulentas como las estrellas de Rock*. Madrid: El Pais.

Childs, G. (1995). Rudolf Steiner Vida y Obra: una biografía ilustrada. Buenos Aires: Editorial Antroposófica.

Childre, D. and Martin, H. (2000). *The Heartmath Solution*. New York: HarperCollins Publishers.

Childre, D. Martin, H. Rozman, D. McCarty, R. (2016). *Heart Intelligence: Connecting with the Intuitive Guidance of the Heart*. Cardiff, California: Waterfront Digital Press.

Dispenza, J. (2007). *Evolve your Brain*. Deerfield Beach, Florida: Health Communications, Inc.

Doidge, N. (2007). *The Brain that Changes Itself*. New York: Penguin.

Dayton, T. (2013). *Tian Dayton: One Foot in Front of the Other*. Deerfield Beach, Florida: Health Communications, Inc.

Duque, J. (2013). Historia de los conservatorios de música e instituciones afines. Barcelona: ESMUC.

Derbez, P. (2015). *El Músico Consciente*. Mexico City: EMDEMUS.

Edwards, S.D and Edwards, D.J., (2018). An empirical and experiential investigation into the contemplation of joy. HTS Theologies Studies/Theological Studies 74 (1) 4746.

Ferreyra, H. & Pedrazzi, G. (2007). *Teorías y enfoques psicoeducativos del aprendizaje*. Mexico City: Ediciones Novedades Educativas de México.

Garello, M. (2016). *Emociones y pensamientos negativos y sus efectos en el cuerpo*. La vida Lúcida.

Gaspar, N. A. (2012). Estrategias de Enseñanza Basada en Aprendizaje Significativo. Revista electrónica en Ciencias Sociales y Humanidades Apoyadas por Tecnologías, 1(1), 35-54.

Goethe, W. (2023) 70 Inspirational quotes from Johann Wolfgang von Goethe. Retrieved from: https://www.readhoot.com/johann-wolfgang-von-goethe-quotes/

Goldstein, B. (2016). *The Secret Language of the Heart.* San Antonio, Texas: Hierophant Publishing.

Goleman, D. (2005). *Emotional Intelligence.* New York: Random House.

Guerri, M. (2020). *20 frases de J.S. Bach.* Valencia: Psicoactiva.

Iborio, E. (2017). *El David de Miguel Angel.* Santiago de Compostela: Historia/Arte.

Iyengar, B. K. S. (2015). *Light on Yoga.* London: HarperCollins.

Jung, C. & Wilhelm, R. (1931). *El secreto de la flor de oro.* Bogotá: Editorial Solar LTDA.

Jaramillo, N., Mercedes, L., Gallardo, S. & Patricia, V. (2014). La metacognición y su aplicación en herramientas virtuales desde la práctica docente. *Sophia, Colección de Filosofía de la Educación,* (16). 299-313.

Kesselman, S. (2002). *El Paradigma Corporal en las Nuevas Pedagogías.* Barcelona: ESMUC.

Kleiman, V. (2012). *Reflexiones sobre las formas de trabajar el cuerpo.* Barcelona: Observatorio de Danza y Estudio del Movimiento.

Kleiman, V. (2019). *Reflexiones y acciones en el tiempo de la improvisación.* Barcelona: ESMUC digital.

Levy, Daniel. (1986) *Eufonia.* Cassiopeia Editrice.

Lipton, B. (2005). *The Biology of Belief.* Felton, California: Mountain of Love.

Ma, Yo-Yo (2018). *Music Happen between the notes.* Retrieved from: www.onbeing.org.

McCarty, R, Atkinson, M, Rein, G and Watkins, A. (1996). *Music enhances the effect of positive emotional states on salivary IgA.* https://www.researchgate.net/publication/229965927_Music_enhances_the_ effect_of_positive_emotional_states_on_salivary_IgA/link/5c7aabd592851c6 9504ee6b9/download.

Morgenstern, S (1956) *An Anthology of Composers' Writings from Palestrina to Copland.* Pantheon.

Morris, Steven M. (2010). *Achieving Collective Coherence: Group Effects on Heart Rate Variability Coherence and Heart Rhythm Synchronization.* Alternative Therapies in Health; Medicine, A Peer-Reviewed Journal, 16(4): 62-72.

Nepil, H. (2017). *Dealing with Stage Fright.* London: BBC Magazine.

Nodhia, A. (2018). *Depression And the Composer: Rachmaninoff's Story,* Northwest Public Broadcasting.

Olsen, M. (2009). *Musician's Yoga.* Boston: Berkeley Press.

Ortiz Brugués, A (2008). Music Performance Anxiety: A Review of the Literature. Unpublished doctoral thesis. Freiburger Institut fur Musikemedizin. Freiburg: Albert-Ludwigs-Universitat Freiburg I. Br.

Pérez, A (2016). Cinco razones por las que todo músico debe meditar. Retrieved from: https://www.aninamasana.com/es/cinco-razones-musico-conviene-meditar.

Perlman, I (2023). Practising Tips from Itzhak Perlman. *Practising the Piano.* Retrieved from: https://practisingthepiano.com/practice-tips-itzhak-perlman/.

Piaget, J. (1936). *Origins of Intelligence in the Child.* London: Routledge and Kegal Paul.

Pozo, J, I. (2006). *Teorías cognitivas del aprendizaje.* Madrid: Ediciones Morata, S.L.

Rodríguez, M.L. (2008). *La teoría del aprendizaje significativo en la perspectiva de la psicología cognitiva.* Barcelona: Editorial Octaedro.

Santa Cecilia, M. (2013). *La voz de la Naturaleza.* Berlin: Made for Minds.

Salmon, P. (1990). A Psychological Perspective on Musical Performance Anxiety: A Review of the Literature. *Medical Problems of Performing Artists,* 5 (1), 1-11

Suzuki, S. (1987). *Mente Zen, mente de principiante.* Buenos Aires: Editorial Estaciones.

Schopenhauer, Arthur. (1998) *Pensamientos, palabras y música,* Editorial EDAF.

Steiner, Rudolf. (1963) *Teosofía,* Editorial Antroposófica

Tolle, E. (2004). *The Power of Now.* Novato, California: New World Library.

Watson, J. (2017). *Behaviorism.* New York: Routledge.

Zander, R and Zander, B. (2002) *The Art of Possibility.* New York: Penguin.

Zaragoza, J. (2017). *Bases Psico pedagógicas.* Barcelona: ESMUC PW.

Zarza, F. J., Casanova, O. Orejudo, S. (2016) *Estudios de música en los conservatorios superiores y ansiedad escénica en España.* Madrid: Revista Electrónica Complutense de Investigación en Educación Musical-RECIEM.